THE AI LINKEDIN ADVANTAGE:

UNLEASH THE POWER OF AI AND DOMINATE THE COMPETITION

BY AL KUSHNER

The AI LinkedIn Advantage

Unleash the Power of AI and Dominate the Competition

Disclaimer

This book is intended to provide general information and insights about leveraging artificial intelligence for professional success, specifically on LinkedIn. The results discussed in this book are not guaranteed, as outcomes may vary based on individual circumstances, skill level, and effort applied.

The strategies and recommendations outlined herein are intended for informational purposes only. The author and publisher make no representations or warranties of any kind regarding the completeness, accuracy, or applicability of the content. Use of the information is at your own risk. The author and publisher disclaim any liability for any direct or indirect loss or damage arising from the application of the advice or tools described in this book.

Published by: SCR Media Inc

Box 7103, Delray Beach, FL 33482

2025

ISBN: 978-1-63227-347-5

Printed in USA

Unlock Your LinkedIn Potential with 100 Expert-Crafted ChatGPT Prompts

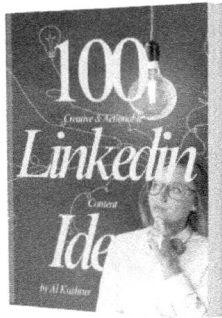

Are you struggling to keep your LinkedIn profile active and engaging? Do you find it challenging to come up with fresh ideas for posts, messages, or professional content? Say goodbye to writer's block and inconsistent engagement with our free guide, **100 Actionable & Creative Linkedin Content Ideas.**

This exclusive guide is your ultimate solution for boosting creativity and efficiency in your LinkedIn strategy. Whether you want to create compelling posts, write impactful messages, or establish yourself as a thought leader, these versatile prompts provide endless inspiration to take your LinkedIn game to the next level.

What's Inside the Guide?

- Engaging Post Ideas: Get ready-to-use prompts to create motivational, educational, and thought-provoking posts that capture attention.
- Networking Made Easy: Draft personal messages and outreach notes that strengthen your professional relationships.
- Personal Branding Boosters: Share your values, career highlights, and expertise with confidence and creativity.

- Thought Leadership Inspiration: Publish impactful articles and content to establish yourself as an industry expert.
- Job-Search Support: Craft messages and posts to stand out to recruiters and employers.

Why Download This Guide?

- Save time brainstorming and focus on building meaningful connections. Increase likes, comments, and shares on your posts with highly engaging content.
- Position yourself as a trusted voice in your industry. Strengthen your personal or company brand effortlessly. Gain insights into how to maximize LinkedIn's potential for professional growth.

Whether you're a professional seeking to elevate your LinkedIn profile, a marketer aiming to enhance brand visibility, or a job seeker looking to stand out, this guide has something for everyone. The prompts are actionable, adaptable, and easy to personalize, no matter your goals.

Grab Your Free Copy Today!

Don't miss this opportunity to transform your LinkedIn strategy and start achieving your professional goals. Download our 100 Actionable & Creative Linkedin Content Ideas.now and get ready to build stronger connections, deliver engaging content, and stand out in the professional world. [**Download the Free Guide Now**]

Table of Contents

Introduction

Linkedin has become more than a platform for professionals—it's a dynamic arena where careers are built, businesses thrive, and brands are established. But in an increasingly competitive digital landscape, standing out requires more than just a polished profile and occasional posts. It demands strategy, precision, and the ability to connect with the right people at the right time.

This is where artificial intelligence (AI) steps in. "The AI LinkedIn Advantage" is your gateway to harnessing cutting-edge AI tools and techniques to revolutionize your LinkedIn presence. This book is designed to empower professionals, entrepreneurs, and job seekers alike to leverage AI for personal branding, strategic networking, and content that captivates. It's about giving you the ultimate edge on a platform that rewards innovation and engagement. Through actionable insights, case studies, and expert tips, this book will show you how to dominate the competition and achieve your goals on LinkedIn like never before.

Get ready to transform your LinkedIn strategy and discover how AI can unlock unprecedented opportunities. Whether you're looking to expand your network, generate leads, land your dream job, or amplify your brand, this book will give you the tools to make it happen.

This book is not just a guide—it's a roadmap to elevate your professional presence and achieve unparalleled success in an AI-driven world. Master the AI LinkedIn Advantage and unlock opportunities you never thought possible.

Bonus
Download

SCAN ME

Chapter 1

Introduction to the AI LinkedIn Revolution

The professional world is in the midst of a seismic shift—one driven by the rapid advance of artificial intelligence (AI). From automating mundane tasks to predicting outcomes with remarkable precision, AI has transformed how we work, interact, and achieve our goals. On LinkedIn, a platform built for professionals to connect, collaborate, and grow, AI is not just a tool but an essential game-changer redefining success.

This chapter sets the stage by exploring how AI has revolutionized professional networking. We begin by tracing the rise of AI, detailing how it has moved from being a niche technology to an everyday tool accessible to individuals and businesses alike. Next, we examine why LinkedIn—one of the most dynamic and influential platforms in the professional space—is uniquely positioned to maximize AI's capabilities. With its robust data ecosystem, global reach, and continuously evolving features, LinkedIn is the perfect playground for harnessing the power of AI.

The chapter dives into how AI is unlocking new opportunities for professionals. Whether crafting laser-focused networking strategies, optimizing profiles to attract the perfect connections, or even predicting the success of a job application, AI is making the impossible possible. For entrepreneurs and businesses, AI-driven insights on LinkedIn can identify untapped markets, spotlight high-value leads, and guide more effective customer engagement.

Adapting to these technological changes is no longer optional; it's imperative. The traditional methods of profile polishing and generic networking strategies don't cut it anymore. With AI in play, the rules have changed. It's about working smarter, not harder. This chapter emphasizes the importance of pivoting to an AI-driven mindset and adopting innovative tools to stay ahead of the curve.

By the end of Chapter 1, readers will clearly understand why the AI revolution on LinkedIn is so significant. They'll feel inspired to accept and eagerly adopt AI as a central element of their LinkedIn strategy. It's time to step into a future shaped by AI and dominate the competition with tools and techniques that were unimaginable just a few years ago. This is the beginning of your transformation—welcome to the AI LinkedIn Revolution.

The Rise of Artificial Intelligence in Professional Networking

Artificial Intelligence (AI) is revolutionizing professional networking, and LinkedIn has become a leading platform where this transformation is taking shape. With its robust data ecosystem and cutting-edge algorithms, LinkedIn is no longer just a digital resume space—it's a dynamic engine for career growth, networking, and innovation. AI's integration into LinkedIn has made it an indispensable tool for professionals and businesses alike, enabling more efficient, personalized, and impactful interactions.

How AI is Reshaping LinkedIn

AI has enhanced nearly every aspect of LinkedIn, turning it into a more robust and tailored platform for users. Here's how this transformation is happening:

1. **Personalized Connection Recommendations**

   LinkedIn's "People You May Know" feature uses machine learning to analyze factors such as shared connections, industries, and everyday skills. This helps users discover highly relevant individuals, whether they're potential collaborators, mentors, or clients. AI simplifies building a strategic, high-value network.

2. **Smart Content Curation**

   LinkedIn's AI algorithms analyze user interactions—likes, shares, comments—to present tailored content on the feed. Professionals now see posts, books, and insights that align with their goals, optimizing time spent on the platform and keeping them informed about key trends in their industry.

3. **Job and Career Matchmaking**

   AI-driven tools like LinkedIn's Jobs feature adapt to users' profiles and preferences, uncovering opportunities highly relevant to their experience. This translates into fewer random searches and more targeted applications for job seekers. Recruiters also benefit as AI highlights the best-matching candidates quickly, streamlining the hiring process.

4. **Skill Assessments and Insights**

   LinkedIn's AI-based skills assessments allow professionals to test and showcase their expertise. Bypassing these tests, users can increase the visibility of their profiles in searches conducted by recruiters or collaborators. AI also suggests relevant courses through LinkedIn Learning to help users stay competitive.

5. **Predictive Messaging Tools**

   Personalized outreach has become easier with AI tools suggesting conversation starters or drafting messages based on recipient profiles. By tailoring communication, users can make stronger connections faster. Additionally, for follow-ups, AI prompts actions based on a user's activity, removing the guesswork from staying engaged.

AI Technologies Powering LinkedIn

Several cutting-edge AI technologies are at the forefront of LinkedIn's evolution:

- **Natural Language Processing (NLP):** This enables LinkedIn's smart replies and personalized messaging features, helping users respond more effectively without losing authenticity.
- **Machine Learning Algorithms** deliver tailored recommendations for jobs and connections and feed content based on a user's activity and preferences.
- **Sentiment Analysis** helps LinkedIn adjust its algorithms to prioritize more engaging and positive interactions, ensuring users find content that resonates.

Benefits of LinkedIn's AI-Powered Features

AI on LinkedIn comes with significant advantages for professionals and businesses:

- **Efficiency:** AI saves users time by tailoring job matches, recommending ideal connections, and showing the most relevant content.
- **Enhanced Visibility:** By optimizing posts and profiles using AI-driven insights, professionals can reach their target audiences more effectively.
- **Opportunity Creation:** AI opens doors to opportunities users might not have discovered otherwise, such as new connections, unlisted job openings, or niche communities.

- **Data-Driven Decisions:** AI analytics enable professionals and businesses to refine their strategies with actionable insights into post performance, audience engagement, and profile visits.

Challenges and Ethical Considerations

Despite its benefits, AI on LinkedIn presents challenges that require attention:

1. **Privacy Concerns:** AI relies on extensive use of personal data, necessitating transparency and ethical considerations to maintain user trust.
2. **Over-Automation:** While AI enhances efficiency, an over-reliance on it can make interactions feel impersonal or robotic—eroding the human touch in networking.
3. **Bias in Algorithms:** AI tools can reflect existing biases in their training data, potentially leading to inequity in job matching or visibility for specific users and groups.

Unlocking LinkedIn's AI-Powered Potential

The rise of AI on LinkedIn is a definitive shift in professional networking. By adopting these tools and fine-tuning their strategies, users can harness the platform's full potential. Balancing automation with authenticity and staying informed about ethical AI use will be key to succeeding in this AI-driven era.

Ultimately, AI on LinkedIn is not just about keeping up with the competition—it's about forging ahead with innovative networking and professional growth approaches. As we continue this AI-powered journey, users who leverage these advantages will find more opportunities and achieve more tremendous success than ever before.

Why LinkedIn is the Perfect Platform to Leverage AI

Artificial Intelligence (AI) has revolutionized many aspects of our lives, from how we shop to the way we learn. LinkedIn stands out as the unparalleled leader in integrating AI technologies among professional networking and career advancement platforms. Whether you're an individual seeking career growth, a recruiter searching for the ideal candidate or a business looking to generate leads, LinkedIn's unique ecosystem provides the perfect foundation for leveraging AI effectively. Let's explore the features that make LinkedIn an ideal AI-driven platform, the applications of AI on the platform, the benefits it delivers, and the challenges it presents.

The Unique Features That Make LinkedIn AI-Ready

LinkedIn's dominance in the world of professional networking is no accident. Its structure, scale, and purpose make it inherently compatible with AI technology. Here's why:

1. Data-Rich Ecosystem

LinkedIn operates on a treasure trove of professional data. With over 900 million users worldwide, LinkedIn houses detailed professional profiles that include information on skills, experience, education, industries, company roles, and more. This vast data pool provides fertile ground for AI algorithms to work their magic. The more prosperous and more comprehensive the data, the better an AI system can analyze and generate insights for personalized user experiences.

2. Professional Focus

Unlike broader social media platforms, LinkedIn is entirely focused on professional growth and development. Its users are not on the platform to share holiday photos or casual updates; they're there to build meaningful professional relationships, search for career opportunities, scout talent, or grow their businesses. This clear focus enables LinkedIn to leverage AI with purpose, delivering tools that cater directly to professional needs.

3. Global Reach

LinkedIn's global footprint spans professional communities of all industries and sectors. This universality allows AI tools on LinkedIn to cater to diverse needs, whether it's connecting a software engineer in India with a job in Silicon Valley or helping a UK-based recruiter find top marketing talent in Asia. Its scale ensures that AI tools can access an immense variety of data points from which to draw.

4. Dynamic User Engagement

The platform continuously evolves with features like posting updates, joining groups, participating in events, conducting polls, and sharing books. These engagement-driven aspects provide AI with live data to assess user behavior. This dynamic activity fuels AI's ability to create proactive recommendations for connections, job postings, and relevant content.

5. Robust Integrations and Tools

Through partnerships with tools like Microsoft Dynamics 365 and LinkedIn Learning, this platform has created a cohesive environment that supports professional growth. AI technologies leverage these integrations to augment further LinkedIn's delivery, from advanced behavioral analytics to skill-building opportunities.

AI Applications on LinkedIn

LinkedIn has strategically implemented AI in various aspects to enhance user experience and streamline professional operations. Here's how AI manifests on the platform:

1. Personalized Connection Suggestions

LinkedIn's "People You May Know" feature uses machine learning to analyze your existing network, everyday skills, shared professional groups, and industry affiliations. This tool makes connecting with valuable professionals more straightforward and more efficient.

2. Job Recommendation Engine

AI algorithms analyze user profiles, career interests, and engagement with job listings to surface tailored job opportunities. For instance, job seekers receive suggestions based not just on their skills and experience but also on the likelihood of succeeding in a role. Likewise, recruiters benefit from curated candidate pools that match the role's specific requirements.

3. Content Discovery and Engagement

AI curates content for users based on their interactions with posts, books, and groups. This ensures that users are constantly exposed to valuable and relevant information, whether it's industry news, insights from thought leaders, or trending skills.

4. Skills Assessment and Course Recommendations

Skill-based assessments allow users to validate their expertise, boosting their visibility to recruiters. LinkedIn's AI also suggests LinkedIn Learning courses to help fill gaps in knowledge, ensuring users remain competitive in their fields.

5. Analytics for Professional Growth

Through tools like analytics dashboards, AI provides detailed insights into profile performance. It highlights the number of profile views, engagement with posts and books, and audience demographics. Companies can also leverage these insights to track the performance of campaigns and optimize content posting strategies.

6. Intelligent Talent Sourcing

Recruiters use LinkedIn's AI-driven talent solutions to identify suitable candidates for open roles quickly. AI-driven filters can pinpoint candidates with specific qualifications, skillsets, or career trajectories, dramatically saving time and resources.

7. AI-Enhanced Messaging

AI tools help users craft contextual and personalized outreach messages, making professional interactions more effective. Predictive follow-up reminders ensure users maintain communication momentum without dropping the ball.

Benefits of Leveraging AI on LinkedIn

AI integration on LinkedIn offers a range of advantages that enhance user experiences and outcomes:

- **Time Efficiency:** AI automates repetitive tasks such as finding job matches, recommending connections, and scheduling posts, allowing users to focus on higher-value activities.
- **Personalization:** Every user gets a unique experience tailored to their career goals, interests, and interactions on the platform.
- **Greater Reach:** Users can effectively extend their influence to new audiences and untapped markets by leveraging AI insights.

- **Improved Decision-Making:** Powerful analytics provide actionable data that helps individuals and businesses make informed decisions about networking, recruiting, or content strategies.
- **Enhanced Competitiveness:** Using AI tools for skills validation or content optimization ensures users and businesses stay ahead in their respective fields.

Challenges of Using AI on LinkedIn

While AI within LinkedIn delivers tremendous value, it's essential to recognize the potential limitations and challenges:

1. **Data Privacy Concerns**

   AI relies on the collection and analysis of user data. Although LinkedIn takes steps to safeguard this information, users must remain aware of privacy concerns and understand the data policies.

2. **Over-Automation**

   Overusing AI-driven features such as automated messaging could lead to impersonal interactions, potentially harming genuine relationship-building efforts.

3. **Algorithmic Bias**

   AI systems are only as good as the data they're trained on. Biases present in data may inadvertently impact job or connection recommendations, creating an uneven playing field.

4. **Learning Curve**

   Adopting and integrating AI tools into their professional strategies may initially feel overwhelming for some users.

Overcoming the Challenges

To fully harness the power of AI on LinkedIn while minimizing risks, users and organizations should:

- Stay informed about privacy settings and data sharing, customizing them based on their comfort levels.
- Use automation sparingly to maintain authenticity and the human touch in interactions.
- Monitor analytics and recommendations to ensure they align with their goals and proactively address any evident biases.
- Educate themselves about LinkedIn's AI features to adapt and improve their strategies continuously.

Conclusion

LinkedIn's unique ecosystem of professional data, global reach, and goal-focused user engagement positions it as the perfect platform to leverage AI technologies. Whether recommending the career opportunity of a lifetime or suggesting that vital connection that might transform your business, LinkedIn's AI capabilities continue to redefine the boundaries of professional networking.

However, the full potential of AI on LinkedIn lies in the hands of its users. By leveraging the wealth of tools and insights made possible by AI, and approaching networking with a balance of automation and authentic relationships, professionals and businesses can unlock unprecedented opportunities on the world's leading professional platform. The future of LinkedIn is undeniably intelligent—and for those ready to adapt, it's full of promise.

Unlocking Opportunities Through Technological Innovation

Technological innovation has reshaped the landscape of opportunity, transforming how individuals and businesses operate, connect, and grow. From artificial intelligence (AI) to advanced digital platforms, today's innovations are enhancing efficiency and breaking down barriers to create unprecedented possibilities. Whether it's redefining how industries function or unlocking creative potential, technological advancements are a boon for those prepared to adapt and evolve. However, alongside these benefits come challenges, such as ethical concerns and the persistent digital divide, which must also be addressed.

Transforming Industries with Technology

Across various sectors, innovations in AI, machine learning, and digital platforms are creating breakthroughs that were once considered science fiction. Here's a closer look at some industries experiencing monumental shifts:

1. Healthcare

Healthcare innovation has led to monumental advancements in patient care, diagnosis, and medical research. AI-driven diagnostic tools, for instance, are enabling early detection of diseases like cancer and Alzheimer's by analyzing patterns in imaging scans and patient histories with more accuracy and speed than human doctors.

- Wearable devices such as smartwatches track real-time health metrics like heart rate and oxygen levels, giving users insights and allowing doctors to monitor chronic conditions remotely.

- Telemedicine platforms have made healthcare accessible even to remote and underserved populations, especially during the COVID-19 pandemic when physical visits became difficult.

2. Finance

Fintech has revolutionized how individuals and businesses manage money. AI algorithms streamline processes like loan approvals, fraud detection, and personalized financial planning.

- Mobile banking apps enable transactions, investments, and money management with just a few taps.
- Central to cryptocurrencies, blockchain technology has introduced a secure, transparent, and decentralized way to handle global transactions, eliminating reliance on intermediaries.

3. Education

The education sector has undergone a digital transformation with the rise of e-learning platforms and AI-enhanced tools.

- Platforms like Coursera, Duolingo, and Khan Academy have democratized learning, making high-quality education accessible worldwide.
- AI tools, such as adaptive learning systems, tailor materials to an individual's pace and style, optimizing learning outcomes for students of all ages.
- Virtual Reality (VR) and Augmented Reality (AR) transform classrooms by offering immersive experiences, such as virtual science labs or historical site tours.

4. Retail and E-commerce

The retail landscape has been revolutionized by technology, from AI-powered product recommendations to automated warehouses.

- Platforms like Amazon use AI to suggest personalized products, enhance logistics, and predict demand using big data analytics.
- AR tools, such as apps that allow users to virtually "try on" clothes or test furniture placement in their homes, have bridged the gap between physical and digital shopping experiences.

These industries are just the tip of the iceberg; sectors like agriculture, logistics, and entertainment are similarly redefined by rapid technological innovation.

The Benefits of Technological Advancements

1. Increased Efficiency

One of the most apparent advantages of innovation is the improved efficiency it offers. AI and automation reduce time spent on mundane tasks, enabling individuals and businesses to focus on activities that demand creativity and strategic thinking. For example:

- Chatbots handle routine customer service queries, allowing human agents to resolve more complex concerns.
- Automated inventory systems in retail minimize human errors and optimize stock management.

2. Improved Accessibility

Technological advancements are tearing down barriers that once limited access to services and opportunities for many.

- E-learning platforms have brought education to rural and underserved areas, enabling individuals to gain skills and certifications from anywhere.
- Mobile payment systems like M-Pesa in Africa provide financial services to populations traditionally excluded from formal banking systems.

3. Enhanced Creativity and Innovation

AI tools enable individuals and companies to think outside the box, generating entirely new avenues for creativity.

- Platforms like Canva and Adobe Express simplify professional-grade content creation for small businesses and individuals.
- Generative AI tools like ChatGPT and DALL·E assist in content writing, visual design, and brainstorming, allowing ideas to flourish faster than ever.

Challenges of Technological Innovation

Despite its benefits, technological innovation creates specific challenges that cannot be overlooked:

1. Ethical Concerns

While powerful, AI and machine learning often raise ethical questions, including issues of Privacy, consent, and bias.

- Companies that collect and process personal data for AI tools must ensure that user information is handled responsibly and ethically.
- AI systems can perpetuate biases encoded into their training data, potentially leading to unintended discrimination in areas like hiring or lending.

2. The Digital Divide

While technology is creating opportunities for many, there remains a significant gap in access to these advancements. The digital divide—differences in access to technology based on socioeconomic status, geography, or other factors—continues to hinder progress in certain communities.

- Rural areas often lack high-speed internet infrastructure, limiting access to e-learning and remote work opportunities.

- Technological literacy is another barrier, as many individuals are unfamiliar with tools or platforms that could benefit them.

3. Job Displacement

While increasing efficiency, automation and AI raise concerns about job displacement, especially in roles involving repetitive tasks.

- For example, automated checkout systems in retail or robotic process automation in data collection can reduce the need for human labor.
- Workers must focus on reskilling and transitioning into roles that require creativity, emotional intelligence, and problem-solving, which machines cannot yet replicate.

Addressing the Challenges

To fully unlock the opportunities created by technological innovation, solutions to these challenges must be prioritized:

1. Promote Ethical AI Practices

Companies should create transparent algorithms, minimize bias, and adhere to data protection regulations. Ethical frameworks for AI development will ensure that technologies benefit all users equitably.

2. Bridge the Digital Divide

Governments and organizations can invest in infrastructure to ensure that underserved areas gain access to technology. At the same time, free or subsidized digital literacy programs can empower individuals to use these tools effectively.

3. Encourage Lifelong Learning

To prepare workers for the changing landscape, governments, businesses, and educational institutions should provide resources for lifelong learning and retraining. Platforms like LinkedIn Learning or Udemy are excellent examples of accessible professional development tools.

The Road Ahead

Technology will continue to transform the world at an accelerating pace. By anticipating both the benefits and the challenges, individuals and businesses can position themselves to unlock the full potential these advancements offer.

For individuals, staying curious and adaptable will be key. Taking advantage of online learning, maintaining awareness of emerging trends, and upskilling regularly can ensure you remain competitive in a fast-moving world.

For businesses, investing in innovative solutions and balancing efficiency with human-centered practices will allow organizations to thrive while maintaining trust and loyalty among both employees and clients.

Ultimately, technological innovation is not simply a tool; it's a catalyst for growth and evolution. For those ready to seize the opportunities it offers, the future promises a wealth of possibilities limited only by imagination and readiness to adapt.

Chapter 2

Building a Magnetic LinkedIn Profile with AI

Your LinkedIn profile isn't just a digital resume—it's your gateway to opportunities, first impressions, and professional connections. With millions of professionals vying for attention on the platform, the competition has never been fiercer. But here's the good news: AI is revolutionizing how you can craft and optimize your LinkedIn presence, ensuring that you don't just stand out—you magnetize the right opportunities directly to you.

Gone are the days when creating an expressive LinkedIn profile meant spending hours agonizing over the right words or the perfect structure. Today, AI does much of the heavy lifting, empowering you to build a profile that reflects your authenticity while leveraging data-driven insights and cutting-edge strategies. Crafting a compelling summary, choosing the ideal keywords, and structuring your content to appeal to recruiters, potential clients, or collaborators are all made simpler and sharper with AI-powered tools.

Why is this important? Because in the modern professional landscape, your LinkedIn profile is often the first point of contact—a digital handshake that speaks volumes about your capabilities, aspirations, and personality. It's your brand in action, accessible to anyone at any time. Whether you're a young professional starting or a seasoned leader looking to expand your influence, an optimized profile is non-negotiable. And AI provides the key to making it magnetic.

Imagine receiving tailored recommendations for your headline or summary that align perfectly with your career goals. Envision AI-driven keyword optimization that makes your profile irresistible to LinkedIn's search algorithms, pushing you to the top of relevant searches. Think about how AI tools can analyze your industry and suggest content that resonates with your target audience—be it recruiters scanning hundreds of profiles or decision-makers searching for industry experts.

This chapter will guide you through leveraging these AI capabilities to create a captivating profile and transform your LinkedIn presence into a strategic powerhouse. You'll discover how AI takes the guesswork out of crafting profiles, using predictive analytics to ensure every word, accomplishment, and skill works in your favor. But it's not just about algorithms and tools—it's about elevating your brand in a way that connects with real people and real opportunities.

By the end of this chapter, you'll understand how to make every section of your profile count, from your headline to your experience details, powered by AI's ability to amplify your strengths and align them with what matters most to your audience. You'll unlock techniques to make your profile attractive and magnetic—a beacon for the opportunities and connections you genuinely deserve.

Welcome to the next step in your LinkedIn transformation. With AI at your fingertips, it's time to reimagine how you tell your professional story and set the stage for career success like never before.

Analyzing Profile Strength with AI Tools

In today's digital-first professional landscape, your LinkedIn profile is often the first impression you make. It acts as your gateway to opportunities, whether seeking a new job, expanding your professional network, or establishing yourself as a thought leader in your industry.

But how do you know if your profile truly stands out among millions of others? This is where AI tools step in to analyze profile strength and offer targeted strategies for improvement.

AI-powered tools are reshaping how we evaluate and enhance professional profiles, offering unparalleled insights into keyword optimization and engagement metrics. These tools don't just tell you what's missing—they guide you in creating a profile that maximizes your visibility and appeal. Let's take a closer look at how AI evaluates profile strength, the tools and features available, the benefits AI brings to the table, and how to balance its insights with authenticity.

How AI Tools Analyze LinkedIn Profile Strength

AI tools are designed to help you understand the effectiveness of your LinkedIn profile. They do this by assessing multiple aspects that contribute to profile strength. Here's how they work:

1. Profile Completeness

AI starts by analyzing the fundamental elements of your LinkedIn profile to determine how complete it is. For example:

- **Section Coverage**: It checks whether you've filled out key areas like your headline, summary, work experience, skills, and recommendations.
- **Media and Attachments**: AI examines whether you've included supporting multimedia like videos, portfolios, or presentations to make your profile visually appealing.
- **Visual Presence**: AI scans your profile picture and background banner for quality and relevancy, which adds to the credibility and attractiveness of your profile.

Platforms like LinkedIn's Profile Strength Meter use AI to give users an overview of their profile's completeness, categorizing progress into statuses like "Beginner," "Intermediate," and "All-Star."

2. Keyword Optimization

AI tools analyze the keywords in your profile to determine how well they align with industry-specific trends and job market demands. For example:

- **Relevance to Your Industry**: AI evaluates whether your profile contains the right keywords for your target roles, industries, or niches.
- **Searchability**: These tools ensure your headline, summary, and skills are optimized for LinkedIn's internal search algorithms, making it easier for recruiters and potential clients to find you.
- Tools like Resume Worded or JobScan specialize in helping users optimize their profiles with tailored keyword suggestions based on job descriptions or industry trends.

3. Engagement Metrics

AI tools look at how your profile performs in terms of visibility and engagement, including:

- **Profile Views**: How many people visit your profile within a specific timeframe?
- **Connection Relevance**: Are the visitors aligned with your career goals or target network?
- **Content Interaction**: Algorithms assess the likes, shares, and comments your posts generate to gauge how engaging your content is.

LinkedIn's analytics dashboard provides metrics on profile views and post engagement, while third-party tools like Shield AI offer more granular insights into visibility trends.

4. Sentiment and Tone Analysis

Some AI platforms assess the tone and sentiment of your content to determine whether it resonates with your target audience.

- **Tone Appropriateness**: AI ensures your summary and posts strike the right professional tone.
- **Value Proposition**: Advanced AI tools evaluate whether your profile effectively communicates your unique value proposition.

5. Skills and Endorsements

AI tools analyze how effectively your skillset is showcased.

- **Skill Validation**: Does your skill list align with your experience and industry trends?
- **Endorsement Impact**: AI reviews the quantity and quality of endorsements to assess the credibility of your listed skills.
- **LinkedIn's Skills Match:** This tool directly evaluates how well your profile aligns with a job posting, helping you optimize for specific roles.

Benefits of Using AI for Profile Analysis

AI tools offer several advantages that empower professionals to refine their profiles and adapt to changing market dynamics.

1. Personalized Feedback

AI delivers tailored insights that are unique to your profile. Instead of generic advice, you receive specific recommendations—for example,

"Consider adding keywords like 'data-driven marketing' to your summary," or "Add a featured portfolio to showcase your design work."

2. Actionable Suggestions

Most tools don't just highlight gaps; they provide actionable advice for filling them. For instance, if your headline lacks actionable language, the AI might suggest including phrases that make it more results-oriented, such as "Experienced Marketing Strategist Delivering Proven ROI."

3. Efficiency and Speed

AI tools dramatically cut down the time it takes to analyze your profile. Instead of spending hours researching trends and keywords, you can rely on AI to surface recommendations in minutes.

4. Enhanced Visibility

By optimizing keywords, headline structure, and other elements, AI ensures your profile ranks higher in searches, increasing your visibility to recruiters and industry professionals.

5. Measurable Performance

AI tracks the effectiveness of your updates over time. For example, you can measure how adding specific keywords or revamping your summary increases profile views or engagement.

Potential Challenges with AI Profile Analysis

While AI offers a host of benefits, it's essential to recognize and address its limitations:

1. Over-Reliance on AI Recommendations

AI-generated profiles, while optimized, can sometimes lose the personal touch. Following recommendations blindly might make your profile sound robotic or too similar to others in your industry.

2. Lack of Context

AI tools operate based on algorithms and may not fully understand the nuanced aspects of your career story or unique personality. For example, they suggest removing non-technical skills crucial to your role as a leader or team-builder.

3. Algorithmic Bias

AI insights are only as good as the data they're trained on. Tools can sometimes prioritize trendy keywords over genuine authenticity, leading to more generic profiles despite being optimized for search.

4. Privacy Concerns

To deliver accurate insights, AI tools need access to your profile data. Ensure you use trustworthy platforms that prioritize user privacy and data security.

Balancing AI Insights with Personal Branding

To make the most of AI tools while maintaining authenticity, it's essential to strike a balance:

1. Use AI as a Starting Point

Think of AI insights as guidelines, not gospel. Use them to identify blind spots and areas for improvement, but ensure your voice and personality remain central to your profile.

2. Customize Recommendations

Even if AI suggests popular keywords, choose the ones that align with your skills and aspirations. Authenticity will always resonate more than generic optimization.

3. Prioritize Storytelling

Your LinkedIn profile is your professional story—AI can suggest edits, but it's up to you to ensure it reflects your unique career path, achievements, and personality.

4. Stay Updated

AI tools are constantly evolving, as is the professional landscape. Make a habit of revisiting your profile regularly to incorporate new insights and trends.

Conclusion

AI tools for analyzing LinkedIn profile strength transform how professionals optimize their online presence. From keyword suggestions to engagement metrics, these tools offer a comprehensive roadmap for making your profile more visible, appealing, and effective. However, the real magic happens when you combine AI's precision with your personal touch.

By using AI as your ally—not your crutch—you can create a LinkedIn profile that ranks high in searches and leaves a lasting impression on recruiters, clients, and colleagues. After all, the goal isn't just to be found; it's to make meaningful connections that advance your career and personal brand. With AI leading the way and your authenticity as its foundation, the future of professional networking is firmly within your grasp.

Choosing the Perfect Headline and Summary Through AI Recommendations

Your LinkedIn headline and summary are the cornerstones of your professional identity on the platform. They're often the first glimpses recruiters, clients, and collaborators get of your expertise and personality. A compelling headline grabs attention, and a well-crafted summary tells a compelling story of your career. But crafting the perfect ones can feel daunting—how do you stand out yet stay authentic? This is where Artificial Intelligence (AI) is your ultimate guide, offering data-driven recommendations that help elevate your profile while staying true to who you are.

AI tools today are revolutionizing how we create LinkedIn headlines and summaries. By analyzing tons of data and personalizing insights, these tools empower you to leverage the right keywords, maintain an engaging tone, and optimize your profile for increased visibility and impact. Read on to discover how AI can help you craft the ultimate headline and summary, its benefits, and how to balance these powerful insights with your branding.

The Importance of a Strong LinkedIn Headline and Summary

Before exploring the role of AI, it's essential to understand why these two sections matter so much. Your **headline** is more than just your job title—it's a snapshot of your professional identity and value proposition. Think of it as a mini pitch that grabs attention in seconds. On LinkedIn, this is crucial because your headline appears in search results, connection requests, and conversation invites.

Meanwhile, your **summary (or "About" section)** allows you to expand on your story. It allows you to:

- Highlight your accomplishments, skills, and career goals.
- Show off your personality, values, and passions.
- Share how you add unique value to your work—and why people should connect with you.

Together, these elements form the foundation of your brand on LinkedIn. They help you attract opportunities while distinguishing you from the crowded marketplace.

How AI Reimagines Headline and Summary Creation

AI tools can serve as your LinkedIn profile coach, analyzing trends and patterns to guide you in creating an optimal headline and summary. Here's how they work:

1. Keyword Optimization

AI tools identify the keywords most relevant to your industry, skills, and target audience. They analyze market trends to suggest terms that recruiters and prospects are searching for. For example:

- A data scientist might receive recommendations for including keywords like "machine learning," "data visualization," and "AI-driven insights" in their headline or summary.
- A marketing professional could receive terms like "growth strategy," "content marketing," or "SEO expert."

By integrating these keywords, AI ensures your profile ranks higher in LinkedIn's search algorithms, making it easier for the right people to find you.

2. Personalization Assistance

AI tools often collect data from your experience, skills, and goals to suggest tailor-made content ideas. For example:

- They may scan your listed accomplishments and recommend, "Highlight your project where you increased company revenue by 20% in your summary."

- AI can even adjust the tone of the suggestions based on your target audience. For instance, it might recommend a formal tone for corporate roles or a creative tone for design-related fields.

3. Tone Analysis

Tone matters, especially in your summary. Are you coming across as approachable, confident, and professional? AI tools use sentiment and tone analysis to review your writing and suggest refinements. They might flag statements that seem overly technical or suggest adding warmth and relatability. A sample AI prompt might say, "Consider replacing industry jargon here with a more conversational phrase."

4. Headline Recommendations

AI tools like Resume Worded or Grammarly's LinkedIn-specific tools analyze existing profiles in your industry to generate headline templates. For example:

- If you're in IT, it might recommend a headline like "IT Professional Specializing in Cloud Security and Scalable Infrastructure."
- For educators, the tool might suggest something like "Innovative Educator Empowering Students Through Technology-Enhanced Learning."

These suggestions ensure your headline stands out while aligning with your career objectives.

5. Data-Driven Adjustments

AI monitors your profile's performance metrics, such as profile views and message responses, and uses this data to fine-tune its recommendations. If your visibility hasn't improved after using specific keywords or formats, it might suggest alternative approaches.

AI-Powered Tools in Action

Some popular tools offering these insights include:

- **Canva's Docs AI** will generate creative summaries.
- **Resume.io** to optimize headlines with role-specific terms.
- **LinkedIn's "Strength Meter"** to measure headline effectiveness.
- **Writing Assistant AI tools** like Jasper or ChatGPT to refine the language and structure without losing individuality.

Benefits of AI-Driven Headline and Summary Creation

AI isn't just about streamlining the process—it's about unlocking opportunities by helping you create content that truly resonates. Here are some key benefits:

1. Increased Visibility

By ensuring your profile contains the right keywords, AI helps you appear in more searches, increasing profile views and connection requests.

2. Professional Branding Boost

AI recommendations can help you showcase your professional expertise with clarity and authority, aligning your LinkedIn presence with your brand.

3. Time-Saving

AI dramatically speeds up crafting a profile by providing ready-to-use suggestions. You no longer need to agonize over every word choice.

4. Adaptability

If you're switching industries or roles, AI tools can help you quickly adjust your tone and keywords to match your new target audience.

5. Consistency

AI maintains consistency across your headline and summary, ensuring they complement each other and convey a cohesive message.

Potential Challenges of Using AI

Despite its benefits, it's essential to use AI wisely. Here are a few challenges you might encounter:

1. Risk of Over-Optimization

AI may sometimes prioritize keyword-stuffing for search engines at the expense of authenticity, making your profile feel generic or robotic.

2. Loss of Individuality

Overusing AI recommendations can strip your headline and summary of your unique voice and story, leaving it sounding like everyone else's.

3. Over-Reliance

It's tempting to rely entirely on AI, but it should serve as a guide, not a crutch. Balancing AI insights with your judgment is crucial.

4. Ethical Gray Areas

Some AI features may unintentionally promote exaggeration or embellishment in profiles, which can backfire if you cannot meet those expectations in real life.

Tips for Balancing AI Insights with Personal Branding

To get the best of both worlds, follow these strategies:

1. Use AI for Research, Not Writing

Treat AI suggestions as a starting point. Let it structure your ideas and identify trends, but write your summary and headline in your voice.

2. Highlight Authentic Achievements

While AI might suggest generic successes, focus on including specific, authentic accomplishments that reflect your unique value.

3. Keep It Conversational

Use AI to refine your writing, but keep it relatable and conversational. Avoid sounding overly polished or robotic.

4. Test and Iterate

Experiment with different AI recommendations and track how they affect your profile metrics. Regularly update your headline and summary based on the results.

5. Reflect Your Personality

Your headline and summary are an extension of your professional self. Add small touches, like personal passions or anecdotes, to make them stand out.

In Conclusion

AI is transforming the way we craft LinkedIn profiles, making it easier than ever to create headlines and summaries that capture attention, maximize visibility, and speak directly to your audience. However, the secret to success lies in pairing AI's efficiency and precision with your authenticity and creativity. By blending the best of technology and personal branding, you can create LinkedIn content that gets noticed and builds meaningful connections and opportunities.

With AI tools as your collaborator, the perfect headline and summary are just a few recommendations away. Take advantage of this cutting-edge technology, stay true to your professional story, and watch your LinkedIn presence soar.

AI-Assisted Selection of Keywords for Better Searchability

Your ability to stand out among thousands of profiles often hinges on one crucial factor—keywords. Whether you're curating an outstanding LinkedIn profile, optimizing a job application, or even growing your brand, choosing the right keywords is pivotal. But how do you know which words pack the biggest punch regarding visibility and relevance? Enter Artificial Intelligence (AI)—a game-changer in the world of keyword selection.

AI-enabled tools transform how individuals and businesses choose keywords to improve searchability and target the right audience. By analyzing vast quantities of data, these tools provide powerful insights to help you stand out in an increasingly competitive digital space. Below, we'll explore how AI enhances keyword selection, its benefits, potential challenges, and tips to effectively use AI-driven insights without losing your flair.

How AI Enhances Keyword Selection

AI tools go far beyond manual brainstorming by leveraging algorithms and predictive analytics. Here's how they improve the process of keyword selection:

1. Industry Trends Analysis

AI tools analyze current trends and language shifts in your field of expertise. For instance, if you're in the technology sector, AI could alert you when terms like "cloud computing" or "DevOps" are surging in demand. By incorporating these into your profile or content, you align yourself with what's relevant in the marketplace.

2. Competitor Insights

AI breaks down competitor strategies by identifying the keywords that are helping them gain traction. For example, tools like SEMrush or Ahrefs can reveal which terms are driving traffic to high-performing LinkedIn profiles or websites within your niche. You can then adopt similar strategies to boost your visibility.

3. Data-Driven Keyword Suggestions

AI provides dynamic recommendations tailored to your career path and objectives. For example, platforms such as Grammarly or JobScan analyze your profile and compare it to job descriptions or industry benchmarks. Using this information, they suggest high-impact keywords for inclusion in your headline, description, or even post content.

4. Cross-Platform Search Optimization

AI-powered tools don't just focus on LinkedIn; they optimize keywords for searchability across different platforms. For instance, some tools recommend terms that improve your visibility on search engines like Google or job boards like Indeed.

5. Dynamic Adaptation

Unlike static keyword lists, AI tools continuously update their suggestions based on new data. This real-time feedback ensures that your keywords remain relevant, even as industry priorities and algorithms evolve.

AI Features That Stand Out

Here are some of the essential AI features that make keyword selection more innovative and highly effective:

- **Semantic Analysis**: Tools like ChatGPT analyze the context around your keywords to provide recommendations that align with your audience's intent.
- **Competitor Matching**: Platforms like SEMrush highlight the terms your competitors are using successfully, giving you an edge.
- **Content Scoring**: AI programs like Rezi or JobScan compare your profile or resume against ideal formats to score your match rate and recommend improvements.
- **Search Algorithm Understanding**: Some tools analyze the nuances of how LinkedIn or Google algorithms rank profiles and suggest corresponding keywords for optimization.

Benefits of Using AI for Keyword Selection

AI-assisted keyword selection comes with several advantages that can elevate your digital presence. Here's a look at the key benefits:

1. Increased Visibility

Using AI-selected keywords often places your profile higher in search results, boosting your visibility to recruiters, employers, and collaborators.

2. Targeted Reach

AI makes your content more relevant to your specific audience by analyzing their preferences and search behavior. This ensures that the right people are seeing your profile or content.

3. Time Efficiency

Manually researching and selecting keywords can be time-consuming. AI streamlines the process by offering research-backed results in minutes, giving you more time to focus on storytelling and personalization.

4. Staying Ahead of Trends

Because AI tools continuously update recommendations, they help you stay relevant in your industry, even when trends change.

5. Enhanced Personal Branding

By matching the terms your audience values most, AI ensures that your keywords reflect exactly what defines you as a professional, enhancing your image and credibility.

6. Improved ROI

For businesses or professionals running paid ads on platforms like LinkedIn, AI-optimized keywords can maximize your return on investment (ROI) by ensuring your audience finds your services quickly.

Potential Challenges of Relying on AI

While AI provides a wealth of capabilities, it's essential to approach its recommendations critically. Here are some challenges worth considering:

1. Over-Reliance on AI

Mindlessly following AI-generated suggestions without tweaking them could lead to a profile or content that lacks authenticity. Too many buzzwords might make your writing sound mechanical or impersonal.

2. Generic Keywords

AI tools often prioritize high-volume or popularly searched terms, which can make your profile blend in rather than stand out among competitors.

3. Ignored Nuances

AI-powered suggestions sometimes fail to capture the nuanced details of your work history or skills. For instance, a particular accomplishment or niche skill might be overlooked in favor of generic terms.

4. Algorithmic Bias

Remember, AI algorithms are only as unbiased as the data they're trained on. They may favor specific keywords or industries over others, leading to recommendations that might not be fully inclusive.

5. Privacy Concerns

AI tools often access sensitive personal information to offer personalized recommendations. Make sure you're using reputable platforms that prioritize data security.

Balancing AI Insights with Personal Branding

To get the most out of AI while preserving your individuality, you must combine its insights with your expertise. Here's how:

1. Use AI as a Guide

Think of AI as a brainstorming partner, not the final decision-maker. While AI can suggest keywords, make sure they align with your goals, tone, and overall branding.

2. Focus on Unique Value

Supplement AI insights with keywords that highlight your distinctive achievements and skills. For example, instead of just using "project management," you could incorporate "led multi-million-dollar IT transformation projects."

3. Optimize but Humanize

Work AI-generated keywords into statements that remain natural and conversational. Avoid cramming too many terms together or sacrificing readability for searchability.

4. Regularly Update Keywords

The professional landscape constantly evolves, and so should your keywords. Revisit your profile every few months using updated AI suggestions to stay relevant.

5. Experiment and Monitor

Test different sets of keywords to track improvements in profile views and engagement. Use AI tools to measure performance metrics and adjust based on what works best.

In Conclusion

Harnessing the power of AI for keyword selection is a game-changing professional and personal branding strategy. From understanding industry trends to optimizing algorithms, AI tools provide you with precision and efficiency in crafting a visible and appealing online presence. However, to truly stand out, you must go beyond buzzwords and infuse your unique story, voice, and expertise into the process.

By treating AI as a collaborator rather than a crutch and balancing its insights with your vision, you'll create a algorithm-friendly and authentically you profile. Whether seeking new career opportunities, growing your business, or establishing thought leadership, AI-assisted keyword selection can position you as a top contender on platforms like LinkedIn and beyond.

Profile Picture Optimization Using AI

Your profile picture is the visual handshake of your online presence. It's your first impression on platforms like LinkedIn, and its impact shouldn't be underestimated. A great profile picture has the power to attract more views, increase connection requests, and inspire trust in potential employers or collaborators. But striking the perfect balance between professional, approachable, and authentic can feel overwhelming. Enter Artificial Intelligence (AI), a game-changing tool that makes optimizing your profile picture faster, more innovative, and more effective than ever.

AI-powered tools analyze various aspects of profile pictures, from your facial expressions to the lighting and background. They provide actionable suggestions to make your photo both professional and engaging, helping you stand out in a competitive digital arena. This book explores how AI enhances profile picture optimization, its benefits, challenges, and how to use these tools effectively while staying true to your brand.

How AI Enhances Profile Picture Optimization

AI uses advanced technologies like image recognition, computer vision, and machine learning to critique and optimize your profile picture. Here's how these tools work and what they look for:

1. Facial Expression Analysis

One of the most important aspects of any profile picture is the expression. AI tools analyze your facial expression to ensure it conveys warmth, confidence, and approachability. For example:

- AI might recommend adjusting your smile to appear more genuine.

- Tools like Photofeeler evaluate whether your expression communicates friendliness, competence, or influence.

2. Lighting and Color Balance

Poor lighting can make even the best photos look unprofessional. AI tools assess the lighting in your photo to ensure it enhances clarity and brings out natural skin tones. For example:

- They might suggest increasing brightness or contrast to make you stand out from the background.
- Some tools use advanced filters to correct shadows or uneven lighting.

3. Background Optimization

AI tools evaluate the background of your profile photo to see if it aligns with a professional setting. For instance:

- They may suggest blurring backgrounds to shift focus entirely onto you.
- Advanced tools like remove.bg can edit or replace busy, distracting backgrounds with clean, neutral ones that enhance the picture's professionalism.

4. Composition and Cropping

AI helps with framing and composition by analyzing whether your face is centered and appropriately cropped. It ensures your face occupies the right photo proportion without being too zoomed in or too far away.

5. Clothing and Presentation

While AI can't choose your wardrobe, it can analyze your clothing in the profile picture to ensure you appear polished and professional. It may recommend neutral colors or suggest changing outfits if patterns are too loud or distracting.

6. Visual Appeal Scoring

Some AI tools, like Snappr Photo Analyzer, score your profile picture on attributes like clarity, competence, and trustworthiness. These scores help you understand how others might perceive your photo and where there's room for improvement.

AI-Powered Tools in Action

Several AI tools stand out in the realm of profile picture optimization:

- **Photofeeler** helps you test how others perceive your expressions, attire, and professionalism.
- **Remove.bg** removes distracting backgrounds and replaces them with neutral tones or virtual office settings.
- **Canva's Magic Resize** feature ensures cropping dimensions are aligned with platform requirements.
- **Snappr** measures a photo's quality and provides actionable recommendations to improve its impact.

Benefits of Using AI for Profile Picture Optimization

Whether you're an individual professional or a business owner, AI-assisted profile picture optimization offers several advantages:

1. Increased Engagement

Profiles with high-quality pictures receive more views, connections, and messages. AI helps ensure your picture is attractive and aligned with what audiences expect in a professional setting.

2. Enhanced Professional Appeal

AI ensures your photo communicates confidence and credibility by tweaking elements like lighting, cropping, and background. This helps potential employers, clients, or collaborators take you seriously.

3. Time-Saving Convenience

Manually reviewing or editing multiple photos can take hours. AI tools analyze and suggest easy, actionable improvements within minutes, streamlining the process immensely.

4. Objectivity

When we review our pictures, personal biases can cloud our judgment. AI removes these biases by offering objective evaluations based purely on data and trends.

5. Adaptation to Platform Standards

Different platforms have varying requirements for profile pictures (e.g., LinkedIn tends to favor close-ups, while Instagram might prioritize creativity). AI tools adjust the cropping and composition to optimize your picture for specific platforms.

6. Broad Accessibility

With the rise of online tools and mobile apps, AI-powered profile optimization is more accessible than ever, catering to users with varying budgets and technical expertise.

Challenges of Using AI for Profile Picture Optimization

While AI presents a wealth of opportunities, there are challenges to address to ensure its use aligns with your branding:

1. Maintaining Authenticity

AI tools often suggest standardized changes that may inadvertently strip your picture of individuality. Over-editing could lead to a polished photo that feels distant or impersonal.

2. Overdependence on Technology

Relying solely on AI recommendations risks creating a profile picture that feels mechanical or overly curated. Your audience values authenticity, which AI cannot replicate entirely.

3. Privacy Concerns

Uploading images to AI platforms raises privacy issues, especially if these platforms store your photos. Always choose services with strict privacy policies to ensure your data remains secure.

4. Limited Cultural Context

AI tools may not always understand the cultural or industry-specific nuances that affect how your photo is perceived. For example, specific attire or expressions might be ideal in one context but may not resonate in another.

5. There's No Substitute for Real Photography

While AI can improve existing images, it cannot replace the value of a high-quality photo explicitly tailored to your brand. Professional photographers still bring an irreplaceable human element to the table.

Tips for Balancing AI Insights with Personal Branding

To make the best use of AI in optimizing your profile picture while retaining authenticity, consider the following tips:

1. Select a Baseline Photo Carefully

Start with a photo that already aligns with your career goals. Choose one that shows you in a clean setting, well-dressed, facing forward with a clear expression, and in a clean setting.

2. Use AI as a Guide, Not a Rulebook

Take AI recommendations as helpful suggestions, but apply your judgment. Preserve elements that highlight your personality, such as a unique color in your outfit or a natural expression.

3. Customize for Your Industry

Adjust your photo to align with expectations in your field. For example, a more formal tone might be ideal in finance, while a relaxed backdrop could suit a creative role.

4. Test Different Versions

Upload variations of your photo to tools like Photofeeler or even survey colleagues for feedback. This helps ensure you're not over-editing or under-utilizing AI recommendations.

5. Prioritize Privacy

Only use AI tools that guarantee the safety of your uploaded images. If in doubt, research data policies or stick to localized editing software rather than cloud-based platforms.

6. Regularly Update Your Profile Picture

Your professional image evolves, and so should your profile picture. Revisit your photo every couple of years to ensure it represents your current self and adapts to changing trends.

In Conclusion

AI is redefining how professionals approach profile picture optimization, offering insights that were previously difficult to obtain. By analyzing elements like facial expressions, lighting, background, and composition, these tools can help you craft a picture that stands out in crowded platforms like LinkedIn. However, the most impactful profile pictures blend the precision of AI recommendations with the authenticity of personal branding.

Remember, while AI can enhance your picture's technical quality, your personal story, values, and personality leave a lasting impression. By striking the perfect balance, you can create a profile picture that attracts the right opportunities and inspires genuine connections. With the right tools and thoughtful execution, your optimized profile picture can become one of the most potent assets in your professional toolkit.

Chapter 3

Personal Branding in the Age of AI

Personal branding has become more than just a buzzword—it's now a vital tool for career growth, professional recognition, and meaningful connections. Whether you're looking to climb the corporate ladder, build a business, or establish yourself as an industry authority, your brand sets you apart. But in an era dominated by technology, how we craft and share that brand is evolving at a staggering pace. Welcome to the age of AI, where cutting-edge tools are redefining how we tell our stories and connect with the world.

The fusion of artificial intelligence and personal branding opens a world of opportunities. AI doesn't just streamline your efforts; it amplifies them. Using AI, you can now unlock insights into your audience's preferences, receive data-driven recommendations to perfect your tone and messaging and create optimized content that increases your reach and impact. AI tools enable you to move beyond guesswork, offering precision and strategy that was once out of reach. Imagine being able to tailor every post, headline, or book for maximum engagement or to predict audience reactions with uncanny accuracy—these aren't futuristic fantasies anymore; they're realities available at your fingertips.

However, this new technological frontier comes with its own set of challenges. While AI can assist in amplifying your voice, it's up to you to ensure it doesn't overshadow your authenticity. After all, personal branding is about being yourself, not a hollow replica of trends or algorithms. Your unique story, experiences, and values are the heart of your brand. When merging AI with your branding strategy, maintaining this core authenticity will make your efforts resonate.

Throughout this chapter, we'll explore the evolving landscape of personal branding in the context of AI. We'll uncover how you can use AI tools to unlock actionable insights, improve engagement strategies, and make a lasting impression. More importantly, we'll discuss how to balance leveraging technology and staying true to your identity. Prepare to redefine your branding in ways you've only imagined as we guide you through this exciting intersection of innovation and self-expression. The future of personal branding is here—and it's more innovative, more efficient, and more impactful than ever before.

Understanding the Core Elements of Personal Branding

Personal branding is no longer just a term reserved for celebrities or entrepreneurs; it has become a critical tool for everyone looking to build their professional reputation and create opportunities in today's interconnected world. Whether you're a job seeker, a freelancer, or a business professional, how you present yourself to the world defines how others perceive your expertise, values, and mission. But what makes a personal brand genuinely impactful? The answer lies in understanding its core elements.

By focusing on authenticity, consistency, and value proposition, you can build a personal brand that stands out and resonates deeply with your audience. These components are the foundation upon which powerful personal brands are built, enabling you to leverage personal connections and digital platforms to their fullest potential. Here's an in-depth look at the critical elements of personal branding, supported by examples, strategies, and actionable advice.

The Core Elements of Personal Branding

1. Authenticity

At its heart, personal branding is about being true to yourself. An authentic personal brand reflects your genuine values, beliefs, and personality. People connect with real, relatable individuals, not overly curated personas. Authenticity helps build trust, the foundation of meaningful relationships—whether with colleagues, clients, or followers.

Why Authenticity Matters:

- **Trust and Integrity:** When you're authentic, people are likelier to trust you and associate your name with integrity.
- **Differentiation:** Authenticity highlights what makes you unique. Trying to imitate others dilutes your personal story and limits your potential to stand out.

Example of Authentic Branding:

Gary Vaynerchuk, a well-known entrepreneur and personal branding expert, embodies authenticity. His candid approach, unfiltered communication style, and passion for helping entrepreneurs make him relatable and trustworthy.

Tips for Staying Authentic:

- Reflect on your values and goals. Show the world what drives you.
- Share personal stories that connect with your professional narrative.
- Avoid adopting trends or strategies that don't align with who you are.

2. Consistency

Consistency is the glue that holds your brand together. It ensures that every interaction—online or offline—creates a coherent, recognizable image of who you are and what you stand for. A scattered and inconsistent brand confuses your audience, while one that's steady and focused sticks in their minds.

Why Consistency Matters:

- **Recognition:** Consistently showing up with the same tone, messaging, and visual identity makes it easier for people to recognize your brand.
- **Dependability:** When you're consistent, people rely on you for expertise in your niche, building credibility over time.

Example of Consistent Branding:

Oprah Winfrey is a shining example of consistency in personal branding. Her brand has always focused on inspiration, empowerment, and storytelling, whether through her talk show, magazine, or network. This unwavering focus makes her one of the most trusted and recognizable figures in the media.

Tips for Maintaining Consistency:

- Define your branding elements, including your tone, messaging, and aesthetic, and stick to them.
- Ensure your social media profiles, emails, and in-person interactions align with the image you're building.
- Regularly update your profiles and website to reflect the exact positioning.

3. Value Proposition

Your value proposition is the unique promise you make to your audience. It answers, "What can you offer that others can't?" A strong value proposition demonstrates your expertise and highlights the benefits of working with or following you.

Why Your Value Proposition Matters:

- **Clarity:** It communicates what you stand for and bring to the table.
- **Attracting the Right Audience:** When your value proposition is clear, the people who resonate with your message are more likely to connect with you.

Example of a Clear Value Proposition:

Simon Sinek's tagline, "Start with Why," encapsulates his expertise in leadership and motivation. His value proposition is crystal clear. By engaging with his content, followers know they can gain actionable insights into purpose-driven thinking.

Tips for Sharpening Your Value Proposition:

- Identify your key strengths and align them with the needs of your audience.
- Focus on how you solve problems or add value in ways that are unique to you.
- Craft a short, memorable tagline that encapsulates your core message.

The Role of Digital Platforms in Amplifying Personal Brands

With the rise of social media and professional networking sites, personal branding has become more accessible than ever. Platforms like LinkedIn, Instagram, and Twitter allow you to share your expertise, connect with like-minded professionals, and engage with your target audience globally. However, these platforms also require a strategic approach to ensure consistent and authentic communication.

Key Strategies for Using Digital Platforms:

- **Leverage LinkedIn:** Build a complete profile that reflects your value proposition, post thought leadership content, and expand your professional network.
- **Share on Instagram:** Use visuals to showcase your personality and lifestyle in a way that aligns with your brand values.
- **Engage on Twitter:** Share tips, comment on industry trends, and participate in dialogues to establish thought leadership.

Remember to adjust your content to suit each platform while maintaining consistency in tone and messaging.

Potential Challenges in Building a Personal Brand

While building a personal brand offers immense opportunities but also challenges that must be navigated thoughtfully.

1. Maintaining Authenticity

With the pressure to stay relevant, some individuals fall into the trap of over-curating their online presence. This can make their brand feel staged or impersonal.

Solution: Stay grounded by staying true to your core values and sharing real stories and experiences.

2. Adapting to Changing Trends

The digital landscape changes rapidly, and strategies that work today might not be effective tomorrow.

Solution: Stay informed and agile, incorporating new trends into your branding without losing focus.

3. Avoiding Overexposure

Posting too much or on too many platforms can lead to burnout or cause your audience to disengage.

Solution: Focus on quality over quantity. Share meaningful content that resonates with your audience rather than trying to fill every platform with constant updates.

Tips for Developing a Personal Brand That Resonates

To create a personal brand that connects with your audience and stands the test of time, follow these actionable steps:

1. **Clarify Your Why:** Understand your purpose. Why are you building a personal brand, and what message do you want to convey?
2. **Understand Your Audience:** Identify your target demographic and tailor your branding to their preferences, needs, and values.
3. **Secure Your Online Presence:** Build a professional website or landing page with your portfolio, testimonials, and contact information.

4. **Invest in Content Creation:** Blogs, videos, and posts that solve your audience's problems help build rapport and credibility.
5. **Network Strategically:** Collaborate with others in your industry to expand your influence and credibility.
6. **Measure and Adjust:** Use analytics tools to track the performance of your personal brand and tweak your approach where necessary.

In Conclusion

Understanding the core elements of personal branding—authenticity, consistency, and a clear value proposition—is essential for crafting a brand that stands out and endures. Combining these foundational elements with the power of digital platforms allows you to connect with audiences on a deeper level, build trust, and create opportunities that align with your goals.

While building a personal brand requires time, effort, and strategy, it's also one of the most rewarding investments you can make. After all, your brand isn't just a reflection of your career; it's an ongoing story showcasing who you are and what you stand for. Make it count.

Leveraging AI to Define and Highlight Your Unique Selling Proposition (USP)

For any business, identifying what sets it apart is fundamental to attracting the right customers and standing out in a crowded marketplace. This defining element, often referred to as the Unique Selling Proposition (USP), captures what makes your product or service not just different but genuinely valuable to your target audience. But in a world saturated with data, shifting consumer preferences, and intense competition, crafting a compelling USP can often feel like piecing together a complex puzzle.

This is where Artificial Intelligence (AI) enters the scene. With its ability to process immense amounts of data, generate actionable insights, and predict trends, AI has become a game-changing tool for businesses looking to define and highlight their USPs. By leveraging AI, businesses can refine their unique offerings and position themselves strategically to resonate with their target audience's needs and desires. From analyzing customer feedback to studying competitor performance, AI-powered tools provide businesses with an unprecedented ability to fine-tune their value propositions for maximum market impact.

How AI Assists in Defining Your USP

AI-powered tools can take the guesswork out of developing a USP. By harnessing machine learning and data analytics, businesses can gain previously unattainable insights or require significant manual effort. Here's how AI helps explicitly in this process:

1. Market Trend Analysis

AI can analyze industry trends and consumer data to highlight your target market's emerging needs, wants, and behaviors. Using predictive analytics, AI identifies patterns that point to untapped opportunities.

- For instance, an AI tool might scan millions of social media posts to detect a growing interest in sustainable products. This insight could inspire a brand to highlight eco-friendliness as its USP.

Example Tool: Tools like Google Trends or Sprinklr use AI to provide insights into trending keywords, topics, and sentiment analysis for specific industries.

2. Customer Feedback Insights

AI excels in processing data from customer reviews, surveys, and feedback. Natural Language Processing (NLP) algorithms can dissect thousands of opinions to highlight positive and negative mentions, allowing businesses to better understand what their audience truly values.

- For example, if feedback repeatedly praises your fast shipping, your USP could focus on speed and efficiency.

Example Tool: Platforms like MonkeyLearn or Lexalytics categorize customer sentiments and extract insights from textual data, turning raw feedback into actionable USP elements.

3. Competitor Analysis

AI tools can also monitor competitor activity to uncover gaps or opportunities. By analyzing your competitors' strengths and weaknesses, AI highlights what they are doing well and where they fall short—creating the perfect space for your USP.

- For instance, if a competitor's customers frequently complain about their lack of personalization, you could position your business as the go-to brand for bespoke services.

Example Tool: AI-enabled platforms like Crayon and SEMrush track competitor strategies, including pricing, promotions, and customer sentiment, offering a window into their approaches.

4. Consumer Behavior Insights

AI doesn't just study what your target audience says—it observes what they do. From online browsing habits to purchasing decisions, machine learning algorithms track behavioral patterns to define what appeals most to your audience.

- A business might discover through AI analysis that its audience prefers convenience over cost, prompting them to focus their USP on hassle-free service delivery.

Example Tool: Customer Data Platforms like Amperity or Segment integrate AI to analyze behavior-based personas and preferences.

5. Personalized Value Refinement

AI tools can help businesses test variations of their USP among different audience segments to determine what resonates most. Through A/B testing and real-time feedback, AI ensures the finalized USP aligns perfectly with audience expectations.

Example Tool: Conversion optimization tools like Optimizely use AI to test different messaging, offering data-driven insights to refine your USP strategy.

Benefits of Using AI to Develop and Highlight Your USP

Integrating AI into the USP development process comes with many benefits that can turbocharge your marketing efforts and overall business strategy. Here's why businesses are turning to AI for USP creation:

1. Enhanced Market Relevance

By leveraging AI to analyze trends and behaviors, businesses can ensure their USP aligns seamlessly with current market demands. A well-defined and relevant value proposition increases the likelihood of attracting and retaining customers.

2. Competitive Edge

AI allows you to dig deeper into competitive landscapes and uncover opportunities others might miss. By carving out a unique position in the market, businesses can enjoy a competitive advantage that boosts profitability and brand recognition.

3. Improved Efficiency

Traditionally, refining a USP requires extensive resources and manual research. AI automates much of this work, shortening the process and reducing costs without compromising depth or precision.

4. Data-Driven Decisions

Instead of relying on subjective guesses, businesses can make informed decisions about their USP based on reliable, data-backed insights. This eliminates blind spots and minimizes strategic risks.

5. Precise Targeting

AI ensures that your USP resonates perfectly with your most valuable audience segments by addressing their specific pain points and desires.

6. Adaptability to Change

AI helps brands stay agile by monitoring trends and shifting audience preferences in real-time. This means your USP can evolve alongside your market, keeping it consistently relevant and impactful.

Potential Challenges of Using AI for USP Development

While AI offers significant advantages, businesses should approach its implementation with thoughtfulness to avoid potential pitfalls:

1. Over-Reliance on AI

While AI can provide incredible insights, it cannot replace the human touch required to infuse authenticity into a personal or brand narrative.

Businesses must avoid becoming overly dependent on AI at the cost of genuine human connection.

2. Maintaining Authenticity

AI's recommendations might lean toward data-driven conformities, and over-optimized USPs could come across as generic or insincere. However, the essence of what makes your brand unique cannot be lost in algorithm-based results.

3. Interpreting Data Incorrectly

AI tools provide insights and patterns, but correctly interpreting them relies on human expertise. Without proper understanding, businesses risk crafting a USP that misses the mark.

4. Privacy Concerns

Some AI tools rely on large datasets, like consumer feedback or behavior tracking, which can raise data privacy issues. Always choose ethical AI solutions that prioritize compliance with privacy regulations.

Tips for Bringing AI Insights into Traditional Marketing Strategies

AI insights must work hand-in-hand with traditional branding principles to create a compelling and grounded USP. Here's how businesses can strike the right balance:

1. **Combine Data with Storytelling:** Use AI insights to guide your messaging but ensure your brand's story and vision remain central. Remember, people engage with brands that feel human.

2. **Validate AI Results Manually:** Before finalizing your USP, verify AI-generated insights through traditional research methods, such as focus groups or interviews, to ensure their relevance.

3. **Iterate Through Testing:** Leverage AI tools to test different versions of your USP in real-world scenarios. Pay attention to audience feedback and refine until the ideal message emerges.

4. **Adapt Without Losing Focus:** While trends are essential to defining your USP, avoid pivoting too frequently. Your USP should evolve but remain consistent with your brand's core values.

5. **Educate Your Team:** Ensure team members, especially those in marketing and branding roles, are trained to effectively understand and utilize AI tools.

6. **Personalize Your Approach:** Use AI-powered personalization to tailor how your USP is delivered to individual segments of your audience, ensuring maximum impact without diluting its message.

In Conclusion

AI has revolutionized defining and highlighting a unique selling proposition, unlocking insights that were once out of reach for many businesses. From uncovering buried customer preferences to analyzing competitor strategies, AI brings data and precision to the often intangible craft of personal and company branding.

At the same time, businesses must remember that at the heart of every great USP are core human values—authenticity, creativity, and empathy. By thoughtfully integrating AI insights with time-honored marketing strategies, brands can create compelling USPs that capture attention and foster genuine connections with their audience. With the right balance, you can harness AI to unlock your business's unique value and make your mark in even the most competitive marketplaces.

AI-Driven Insights for Showcasing Skills and Achievements

Your professional reputation is now largely shaped by how you present your skills, expertise, and accomplishments online. Whether you're actively job-seeking, aiming for career advancement, or simply establishing your presence as an industry leader, effectively showcasing your skills and achievements is a vital part of personal branding. But crafting the perfect narrative isn't always easy. Which achievements should you highlight? How should you structure your skillset for maximum impact? And how do you ensure it strikes the right chord with your audience? Enter Artificial Intelligence (AI).

AI tools are redefining how professionals tell their stories on platforms like LinkedIn. By leveraging insights drawn from vast data sets, AI can analyze your profile, recommend improvements, and ensure your content is tailored to professional expectations and search algorithms. With AI's guidance, you can amplify your skills and achievements, attract relevant opportunities, and grow your network. Here's how AI can transform how you showcase your professional journey.

How AI Helps Highlight Skills and Achievements

AI-powered tools provide many benefits for showcasing and optimizing your skills and accomplishments. From profile audits to content suggestions, here are the ways AI can elevate your professional presence:

1. Profile Analysis and Recommendations

AI tools like LinkedIn's "Profile Strength" or third-party platforms scan your profile to assess its completeness and relevance. These tools can identify gaps in your content, like missing keywords, incomplete sections, or unclear achievements.

- For instance, AI-enabled software may suggest including a project under the "Experience" section to ensure your leadership skills are evident.
- It may also highlight discrepancies between your listed skills and the roles or industries you're targeting.

Example Tool: LinkedIn's built-in AI recommends keywords most searched for in your industry while prioritizing sections critical for visibility, such as the "Headline" and "About" summary.

2. Keyword Optimization

AI suggests industry-specific keywords to position your profile higher in search results. It also helps boost visibility by recognizing and recommending terms recruiters and contacts frequently search for.

- For example, if you're an IT professional, AI tools might suggest adding trending keywords like "cloud computing," "data analytics," or "cybersecurity" to your skills list based on industry trends.

Example Tool: Tools like ResumeWorded analyze profiles and resumes for optimized industry phrases that drive engagement and search matches.

3. Achievement Structuring and Visibility

One of the challenges individuals face is quantifying and presenting their achievements compellingly. AI assists in transforming vague mentions into concrete, measurable results.

- Instead of writing "managed a project," AI tools can suggest phrasing like "led a cross-functional team of 10 to complete a $1M project 20% under budget within three months."

Example Tool: Platforms like GrammarlyGO use AI to help individuals improve their wording or presentation, ensuring their achievements stand out with bullet-point clarity.

4. Tailored Summary Creation

Your professional summary is often your introduction to the digital world. AI tools create impactful summary drafts based on your career history and achievements.

- For instance, after analyzing your experience, an AI generator might create a succinct, keyword-rich summary that emphasizes both your leadership qualities and industry-specific expertise.

Example Tool: Jasper AI can help write summaries tailored to your professional tone and goals to make a powerful first impression.

5. Visual Content Optimization

Sometimes, effectively showcasing achievements involves going beyond simple text. AI tools can assist in creating data visualizations, graphs, or infographics that highlight your impact.

- For example, AI can help you design an infographic showing the metric-based growth you contributed to within your organization.

Example Tool: Canva Pro, powered by AI, provides pre-designed templates to visualize achievements like sales results or timeline impact.

6. Real-Time Feedback and Insights

AI doesn't just evaluate static profiles; it provides real-time advice on content like books or posts. If you share an achievement online, AI can help structure and format it for maximum engagement.

- For example, if you post about completing a certification, AI can recommend tips for enhancing the post with hashtags or highlights.

Example Tool: LinkedIn's AI-powered publishing tools analyze your post's tone, engagement potential, and formatting to improve its reach.

7. Comparison with Peers

AI tools can benchmark your profile against other professionals in your field to identify areas for improvement.

- For instance, platforms could suggest additional soft skills or leadership examples based on competitor profiles, helping you stay competitive.

Example Tool: Jobscan compares your profile's alignment to job descriptions, helping you fill gaps.

Benefits of Using AI for Personal Branding

Using AI to showcase skills and achievements comes with tangible benefits beyond improving your profile's aesthetics. Here's how AI can profoundly enhance personal branding:

1. Instant Visibility Boost

AI tools align your profile with platform algorithms, ensuring your skills and experiences appear in the right searches and contexts, increasing your profile's discoverability.

2. Personalized Guidance

Traditional profile-building workshops or guides often use a one-size-fits-all approach. With AI, the recommendations are tailored specifically to your role, industry, and goals.

3. Data-Driven Storytelling

AI uses data as the backbone for its recommendations, meaning your storytelling is polished and supported by relevant trends and market needs.

4. Saves Time

By automating sections like summaries, keywords, and phrasing, AI tools significantly reduce the time spent on editing and updating profiles.

5. Confidence Builder

AI insights empower users to understand how their skills are valued in the professional world, giving them the confidence to showcase them unapologetically.

6. Improved Engagement

An optimized profile with effectively written achievements and skills gets noticed faster by recruiters or peers, leading to increased profile views and opportunities.

Potential Challenges of Using AI

Despite its utility, there are challenges and considerations to keep in mind when relying on AI for personal branding:

1. Over-Reliance on Technology

Overusing AI may result in generic or overly calculated profiles, which could feel impersonal to those reviewing it.

2. Loss of Authenticity

AI often generates "perfect" phrasing, but an over-polished profile risks losing the authenticity needed to connect with others on a personal level.

3. Privacy Concerns

AI tools often require extensive data to provide insights. Safeguarding personal information when using these tools is a critical concern.

4. Limited Contextual Knowledge

While AI understands language and trends, it doesn't always grasp the full context of your experiences, leading to incomplete or irrelevant recommendations.

Tips for Integrating AI Insights with Personal Storytelling

To ensure you strike the right balance, here's how to merge AI-generated insights with your unique personal voice:

1. **Humanize AI Suggestions:** Use AI tools as a foundation, then edit recommendations to align with your personality and communication style.
2. **Highlight Soft Skills:** While AI can focus on technical expertise, remember to interweave your interpersonal skills (e.g., leadership, collaboration) for a holistic story.
3. **Add Narratives:** Turn AI-optimized achievements into stories that look deeper into your impact, struggles, and solutions.
4. **Focus on Authenticity:** Don't overload your profile with buzzwords. Choose language that reflects how you naturally describe yourself.
5. **Keep AI Tools Updated:** Ensure the tools you're using account for the latest trends in your industry to avoid outdated guidance.
6. **Validate AI Results:** Regularly revisit and revise AI-generated suggestions to ensure they align with where you want your professional brand to go.

In Conclusion

AI-powered tools have unlocked a wealth of possibilities for individuals aiming to define and showcase their skills and achievements more compellingly. These tools provide an invaluable edge in the professional world, from optimizing profiles for industry trends to fine-tuning summaries and achievements for impact.

While it's easy to be enchanted by AI's capabilities, remember that your voice, experiences, and authenticity remain the central pillars of personal branding. Use AI as an assistant—not as the sole content creator—to ensure a profile that doesn't just capture attention but inspires trust and connection. By balancing technology with genuine storytelling, you can position yourself for meaningful engagement and opportunities, showcasing what you do and who you indeed are.

Maintaining Authenticity While Integrating AI Tools

The rise of artificial intelligence (AI) has transformed how we communicate, create, and connect. From automating tasks to providing data-driven insights, AI tools have become essential in various personal and professional branding aspects. Yet, as AI's efficiency and convenience grow, so does a critical question—how do we ensure authenticity is not lost in the process?

Authenticity is the foundation of trust and meaningful engagement. People value genuine interactions and relatable messages, whether you're building a personal brand, marketing your business, or connecting with customers. While AI offers powerful tools to amplify your reach and streamline tasks, its automated nature can sometimes risk creating content or responses that feel impersonal or disconnected. The challenge lies in striking the right balance—harnessing AI's capabilities to enhance what you do without overshadowing your authentic voice and values.

This book explores how to integrate AI tools intelligently while maintaining the authenticity that sets you apart.

Why Authenticity Matters in Branding and Communication

Authenticity goes beyond being honest—it's about being relatable, consistent, and aligned with your core beliefs and values. Here's why staying authentic is vital in personal and professional endeavors:

1. Building Trust

People trust genuine people. When your audience senses authenticity, they are more likely to connect with you, whether as a professional, a business, or a brand.

2. Differentiation

Your unique voice, personality, and approach make you stand out. Authenticity helps distinguish you in a crowded marketplace or competitive job landscape.

3. Long-Term Relationships

Authentic connections foster loyalty. Customers and followers are likelier to stay engaged with brands or individuals that resonate with their values and experiences.

4. Human Connection

People connect with other people—not algorithms. Your authentic story and presence create the emotional resonance needed for deep connections.

How AI Can Enhance (But Not Replace) Authenticity

AI tools offer incredible potential to enhance marketing, content creation, and customer engagement—as long as they're used thoughtfully. Below are prominent AI applications that can support authenticity when leveraged correctly:

1. AI in Marketing

AI streamlines analyzing customer data, identifying trends, and optimizing campaigns. For example, AI tools like HubSpot or Salesforce can provide audience insights that allow businesses to target their messaging more effectively.

However, to maintain authenticity, marketers should customize their AI-generated campaigns to reflect their brand voice and connect personally with their audience. For instance, businesses can adapt automated messages to include personalized details and handwritten follow-ups instead of relying solely on prewritten email templates.

2. AI in Content Creation

AI-driven platforms like Jasper or Grammarly are excellent for generating ideas, improving grammar, and structuring content. These tools save time but must not overshadow the personal touch. Integrate your unique perspective, experiences, or tone into AI-assisted work to ensure the message feels authentic and aligned with your audience.

For example, if you're sharing a book or social post, use AI for editing but include personal anecdotes, humor, or reflections that only you could add.

3. AI in Customer Engagement

Chatbots powered by AI are widely used for quick customer responses. They're efficient in answering frequent queries but lack the warmth of human interaction. Striking a balance is key—use AI for fundamental customer interactions while stepping in to handle more complex or emotional concerns personally.

For instance, customer service teams can allow chatbots to answer routine questions but follow up with personalized emails or calls for more involved issues. This blend ensures clients feel valued and heard.

4. AI-Assisted Personal Branding

AI tools like LinkedIn Insights and Canvas personalized templates can analyze your profile performance and help tailor visual or written branding elements. However, avoid over-relying on AI-generated suggestions. Add elements that reflect your unique career path, achievements, and passions to keep your professional persona your own.

Challenges in Balancing AI with Authenticity

While AI offers significant advantages, its integration can pose challenges if not approached carefully. Key concerns include:

1. Over-Reliance on AI

When too much is delegated to AI, the human touch essential for building relationships may be lost. Over-reliance could lead to robotic interactions, generic messaging, or missed emotional nuances.

2. Loss of Personal Connection

AI cannot express empathy, humor, or cultural context the way humans can. People can quickly recognize when something feels overly automated or impersonal.

3. Generic Content

AI optimizes for trends or algorithms, sometimes resulting in cookie-cutter outputs that fail to capture individuality. Audiences may struggle to see the unique qualities that set you apart.

4. Ethical Concerns

There may be ethical ramifications if customers or audiences feel deceived by overly polished or automated interactions. For instance, failing to disclose that AI content was used can undermine credibility.

Strategies for Balancing AI with a Personal Touch

To ensure AI enhances rather than compromises authenticity, here are effective strategies for finding the right balance:

1. Customize AI-Generated Content

Continually review and adjust AI-generated work to align with your voice and intent. Add personal stories, relevant examples, or specific details only you can provide.

2. Use AI for Repetitive Tasks

Leverage AI for tasks like scheduling, grammar checking, SEO optimization, or data analysis while reserving creative and emotional elements for human effort.

3. Be Transparent

When using AI tools, be transparent about their role in your process. For example, clarify when messaging or content was partially AI-assisted, which can build trust and credibility.

4. Test and Iterate

Experiment with different AI setups to find what works without diluting your authenticity. Gather feedback from your audience to understand which efforts resonate most.

5. Integrate Emotion and Storytelling

AI can provide data, but you give the heart. Add emotion, humor, or relatable struggles to the content to create memorable human connections.

6. Focus on Active Engagement

While AI can improve efficiency, allocate time for honest conversations with your audience. Reply personally to comments, messages, or queries to show you genuinely care.

7. Balance Automation with Human Oversight

Deploy AI tools to supplement, not replace, human presence. Whether managing social media accounts or sending newsletters, ensure there's always a human review layer involved.

Tips for Integrating AI While Preserving Originality

Here are practical steps to help you make the most of AI tools without compromising authenticity:

1. **Define Your Core Values**

   Before using AI, clarify what you want your personal or professional brand to represent. Use these values to guide AI-driven projects, ensuring alignment with your overarching mission.

2. **Humanize Data Insights**

   AI-generated data is a great starting point but contextualize it. Turn stats into narratives or insights that directly connect with what matters to your audience.

3. **Maintain Consistency Across Platforms**

   AI can help manage your presence on multiple platforms but ensure your brand tone remains consistent. Authenticity thrives in consistency.

4. **Highlight Collaboration with AI**

   Celebrate how AI complements your efforts rather than pretending it's a behind-the-scenes secret. For example, share how you use AI to brainstorm ideas or analyze data for creativity.

5. **Tailor Audience Interactions**

How AI-based recommendations align with your audience's expectations or preferences. Customize each interaction to build and sustain trust.

In Conclusion

AI can be a remarkable ally in boosting creativity, productivity, and reach—but its full potential lies in its collaboration with human input. Authenticity doesn't come from algorithms but from shared experiences, personal stories, and genuine connections.

Use AI to enhance, not overshadow, your identity. When thoughtfully integrated, AI becomes a tool that amplifies your impact without compromising the personal touch that makes your brand unique. By balancing efficiency with empathy, technology with humanity, and insight with real-world context, you can achieve the perfect synergy between AI innovation and authenticity. Ultimately, staying true to who you are while leveraging the best of what AI offers enables you to thrive in a modern, AI-driven world.

Chapter 4
Networking Redefined with AI Tools

Networking has always been a cornerstone of professional growth. Whether you're looking to land a new job, secure a partnership, or connect with peers in your industry, building and maintaining relationships is crucial. Yet, traditional methods often fall short in the digital age. The sheer volume of platforms, connections, and conversations can make it overwhelming to efficiently and meaningfully engage with others. Fortunately, integrating Artificial Intelligence (AI) redefines how professionals network, making it more thoughtful, personalized, and infinitely scalable.

AI-powered tools are revolutionizing how we connect by analyzing data, predicting patterns, and streamlining communication. From identifying the right people to connect with to optimizing what you say and tracking your engagements' success, AI has opened up new possibilities in networking. However, with these advancements comes the responsibility to ensure that professional interactions remain authentic and human-centered. This chapter explores how AI tools are transforming networking, their benefits, challenges, and best practices for leveraging AI without losing the essence of meaningful connections.

The AI Impact on Networking

AI has turned networking into a high-tech, data-driven process. Traditionally, networking involved face-to-face meetings, business cards, and mutual contacts. Now, AI introduces tools that can identify potential connections with pinpoint accuracy, predict networking opportunities, and even automate aspects of communication. Networking is no longer confined to in-person events or chance introductions. Thanks to AI, it happens across global platforms, cutting through distance and inefficiency.

Here's how AI-powered features are reshaping networking as we know it:

1. Enhanced Connection Opportunities

AI uses vast datasets to help professionals identify who to connect with, providing valuable opportunities that were not previously on their radar.

- **Connection Suggestions:** Platforms like LinkedIn use AI to suggest connections based on shared skills, mutual contacts, or your industry. These recommendations aren't random but are personalized using algorithms designed to increase professional relevance.
- **Industry-Specific Communities:** AI helps users discover niche groups and communities they might not have encountered. For example, it could recommend joining a forum for AI experts or a local entrepreneur network.

Example: Tech startups often use tools like AngelList and Niche.ai, which leverage AI to match them with investors or mentors aligned with their business models or values.

2. Personalized Interactions

AI doesn't just identify whom to connect with—it also tailors how you communicate. By leveraging data on an individual's preferences, interests, or professional history, AI equips you with insights to make your approach more personal and meaningful.

- **Message Optimization:** AI tools can suggest personalized opening lines based on shared connections or mutual interests with a prospective contact.
- **Content Personalization:** Platforms like Crystal Knows offer personality insights based on an individual's publicly available content, helping you tailor your communication style.

Example: Suppose you're preparing to message a company's hiring manager. AI might identify their recent post about workplace diversity and suggest referencing it to spark an authentic conversation.

3. Data-Driven Insights

The ability of AI to process and analyze massive amounts of data allows professionals to make informed networking decisions.

- **Profiling Opportunities:** AI reviews profiles, posts, and activity to determine whether a connection aligns with your goals. For example, it might identify someone as a thought leader in sustainability based on their posts and engagements.
- **Engagement Tracking:** AI tools like Linked Helper analyze the success of your communications, tracking metrics like open and response rates to reveal what approaches work best.

Example: Tools like ZoomInfo provide in-depth information about decision-makers, including job titles and contact information, helping you approach them strategically.

4. Predictive Analytics

AI-powered predictive analytics go beyond real-time insights to forecast future networking opportunities.

- AI can identify trends in professional activities and help you anticipate which connections will be the most valuable for upcoming projects or collaborations.
- Predictive analytics tools can assess who will most likely accept your connection request or engage in follow-up communication.

Example: LinkedIn's Sales Navigator uses AI to detect signals like job changes or industry shifts, notifying users of prime opportunities to reach out.

Benefits of AI in Networking

Integrating AI into networking offers numerous advantages that can significantly enhance professional relationship-building efforts. These include:

1. Efficiency and Time Savings

AI simplifies networking by automating time-consuming tasks like searching for potential contacts, following up, and even scheduling meetings. Instead of spending hours manually researching, AI tools deliver actionable insights in seconds.

2. Broader Reach

With AI, networking is no longer limited to your geographic region or immediate professional circle. AI tools enable you to connect with individuals and groups across industries and continents, expanding your reach far beyond what traditional networking methods allow.

3. Targeted Connections

By analyzing relevant data, AI enables you to focus on high-value relationships that align with your goals. Whether pinpointing influential thought leaders or discovering peers with similar career trajectories, AI ensures you prioritize quality over quantity.

4. Enhanced Communication

AI tools make networking more effective by guiding what to say and when. They help refine your messaging, ensuring it resonates with your audience while remaining professional and engaging.

5. Real-Time Adaptability

AI-powered tools continuously analyze data, adapting recommendations and strategies based on evolving trends. This helps you stay ahead in competitive networking environments.

Challenges of Networking with AI

While AI offers clear advantages for modern networking, it has challenges. Key issues include:

1. Maintaining Genuine Relationships

Connections built purely on data analysis risk feeling transactional or impersonal. People value authenticity and may be skeptical of overly calculated interactions, leading to shallow or unsustainable relationships.

2. Over-reliance on Automation

Excessive reliance on AI for tasks like messaging or follow-ups can strip professional relationships of the human touch they require to thrive.

3. Data Privacy Concerns

AI tools often involve accessing personal or professional data from public sources. Ensuring ethical practices and compliance with data privacy regulations is essential to avoid potential backlash.

4. Algorithmic Bias

AI recommendations are only as unbiased as the data on which they are trained. Relying exclusively on AI could lead to missed opportunities or connections due to inherent biases in algorithms or data inputs.

Tips for Networking Effectively with AI

To successfully integrate AI into your networking efforts without compromising relationship quality or authenticity, consider the following strategies:

1. Strike a Balance

Use AI to augment your networking but ensure that interactions still feel personal. Draft messages with AI assistance, but add your voice and unique perspective.

2. Focus on Quality

AI can connect you with hundreds of potential contacts but focus on fostering a few meaningful relationships. Invest time in personalized interactions that go beyond surface-level communication.

3. Be Transparent

If you're using AI for follow-ups or recommendations, don't shy away from acknowledging it. Transparency builds trust and shows that technology is a tool, not a replacement for your effort.

4. Customize Interactions

Take the data-driven insights AI provides and tailor them to specific individuals. For example, reference their recent work or shared experience instead of sending a generic LinkedIn request.

5. Monitor and Refine Results

Regularly evaluate the success of your AI-assisted networking efforts. Use analytics to assess whether your connections are meaningful and adjust strategies as needed.

6. Prioritize Data Ethics

When using AI tools, ensure you comply with data privacy regulations. Only leverage publicly available information and choose AI platforms committed to ethical practices.

In Conclusion

AI tools have undoubtedly redefined networking, making it more strategic, scalable, and impactful. By leveraging AI, professionals can open doors to opportunities they never knew existed, create personalized connections, and remain up-to-date with emerging trends. At its core, however, AI should enhance human interaction, not replace it.

The key to effective AI-driven networking is balance. Stay genuine, prioritize authentic connections, and use AI to complement—not overshadow—your human efforts. When done correctly, integrating AI into your networking strategy can transform how you connect, grow, collaborate, and succeed professionally.

Using AI to Identify Key Decision-Makers and Influencers

Success in business often depends on your ability to form strategic relationships. Whether you're looking to pitch a product, close a deal, or grow your brand, connecting with the right decision-makers and influencers can make all the difference. Historically, this process required extensive research, networking, and time-consuming trial and error. But with the rise of Artificial Intelligence (AI), identifying and engaging with influential individuals has become faster, more accurate, and more strategic.

AI leverages vast data to help businesses pinpoint key industry players, streamline outreach, and optimize engagement strategies. From analyzing professional networks to tracking social media activity, AI tools uncover valuable insights that guide decision-making and help businesses connect with the right people at the right time. However, like all advancements, AI's use in identifying decision-makers and influencers comes with its challenges, including privacy concerns and the risk of losing personal touch.

This chapter explores how AI can revolutionize the way businesses identify key decision-makers and influencers, the benefits it offers, and how to overcome its potential pitfalls. Most importantly, it provides actionable strategies for using AI effectively to create meaningful, impactful relationships.

The Power of AI in Strategic Targeting

AI excels at processing and analyzing vast amounts of data—something humans cannot do at the same scale or speed. When identifying decision-makers and industry influencers, AI tools analyze patterns and connections across multiple platforms and databases to pinpoint individuals who hold sway in their sectors.

Here's how AI powers strategic targeting in the business world:

1. Mapping Organizational Structures

AI can help uncover who holds decision-making authority within organizations by analyzing public records, company websites, and professional platforms like LinkedIn.

- **Example:** Tools like ZoomInfo or Clearbit provide organizational charts highlighting key individuals, such as CEOs, department heads, or project leads.

2. Tracking Social Media Influence

AI-powered tools analyze social media platforms to identify individuals with significant influence in specific industries based on engagement metrics like followers, shares, and audience demographics.

- **Example:** Social listening tools like Brandwatch and BuzzSumo track trending topics and influencers driving conversations in your niche.

3. Analyzing Content and Communication

AI tools can evaluate published content—such as blogs, books, or social posts—to determine who is leading thought leadership efforts and their areas of expertise and influence.

4. Predicting Emerging Influencers

AI uses predictive analytics to identify rising stars in a field before they become widely recognized. It analyzes factors like the growth rate of their audience, frequency of mentions, and engagement trends.

- **Example:** A PR firm could use AI to discover an up-and-coming tech blogger whose influence is outpacing industry veterans.

Benefits of Using AI to Identify Key Players

AI dramatically enhances the process of locating decision-makers and influencers, unlocking a wide range of benefits for businesses:

1. Efficiency

Traditional methods of identifying decision-makers—such as manual research or unsolicited outreach—can be time-consuming and resource-intensive. AI accelerates this process, delivering actionable insights in minutes rather than hours or days.

2. Greater Accuracy

AI mitigates human error by analyzing large datasets to produce reliable and precise results. It can filter out irrelevant contacts and focus on those who align best with your business goals.

3. Strategic Targeting

AI prioritizes quality over quantity, ensuring you direct your efforts toward individuals with the most impactful roles or platforms. This focus minimizes wasted resources and maximizes ROI.

4. Enhanced Insights

By evaluating data from various sources, AI provides a comprehensive view of decision-makers and influencers—not just who they are but also their motivations, preferences, and pain points.

5. Staying Ahead of Trends

AI's ability to analyze real-time data means businesses can identify upcoming trends and key players before their competitors, keeping them ahead of the curve.

Challenges in Using AI to Identify Decision-Makers and Influencers

Despite the benefits, businesses must address several challenges when incorporating AI into their strategies for identifying key individuals:

1. Data Privacy

Accessing and analyzing data comes with responsibility. Governments and organizations have strict rules regarding data collection and use, and businesses must ensure compliance to avoid legal repercussions.

2. Bias in AI Algorithms

AI tools are only as objective as the datasets they analyze. If the data is incomplete or biased, results may overlook critical segments or overemphasize others, leading to skewed targeting.

3. Over-Reliance on Technology

While AI can streamline the discovery process, human judgment is essential for building genuine and meaningful connections. Over-relying on AI risks reducing outreach to a transactional effort.

4. Maintaining Authentic Relationships

Outreach resulting from AI recommendations can sometimes feel impersonal if not handled carefully, potentially alienating the individuals you're trying to engage.

5. Integration Complexity

Using multiple AI tools requires proper integration and alignment. An uncoordinated system might lead to inefficiency and confusion instead of streamlined communication.

Tips for Effectively Using AI in Engaging Decision-Makers and Influencers

To reap the full benefits of AI while overcoming potential challenges, consider the following strategies:

1. Define Your Goals and Audience

Before using AI tools, establish clear objectives for your outreach efforts. Identify which industries, roles, or types of influencers you need to target to meet your goals.

2. Choose the Right Tools

Not all AI tools are created equal. Select platforms that cater to your needs, such as social listening, data enrichment, or predictive analytics. For instance:

- Use LinkedIn Sales Navigator to identify professional decision-makers.
- Leverage TrendSpottr to find rising influencers in your market.

3. Humanize the Outreach

Pair AI-generated insights with a personalized approach. Instead of sending generic messages, reference shared interests, recent posts, or relevant work that AI tools highlighted.

4. Leverage Data Responsibly

Ensure compliance with data privacy laws like GDPR or CCPA. Use only publicly available data and communicate transparently how you've discovered and intend to use it.

5. Continuously Monitor and Adjust

AI recommendations evolve as new data becomes available. Regularly revisit insights to ensure your outreach efforts remain relevant and impactful.

6. Build Relationships Beyond Transactions

Connecting with decision-makers and influencers is not just about a single campaign or deal. Focus on nurturing long-term, mutually beneficial relationships. Combine AI-driven efficiency with ongoing human interaction to build trust.

7. Balance Automation with Personal Effort

Use AI for repetitive or high-level tasks like identifying prospects or scheduling but ensure meaningful engagement remains human-led.

8. Benchmark Success

Set KPIs for your AI-driven efforts, such as response rates, engagement levels, or partnerships secured. Evaluate performance regularly to fine-tune your strategies.

In Conclusion

AI is transforming the way businesses identify and engage with decision-makers and influencers. AI empowers professionals to make targeted, strategic decisions like never before by providing data-driven insights, streamlining processes, and uncovering new opportunities. However, the true value of AI lies in how it complements human efforts. Combining AI's efficiency with personal authenticity is the key to building long-lasting, impactful relationships.

By adopting the tips and strategies outlined in this chapter, businesses can rise above the competition, forge meaningful partnerships, and ensure their messages land where they matter most. When used thoughtfully, AI is a technological tool and a pathway to smarter, stronger connections in today's dynamic business landscape.

Enhancing Connection Requests with AI-Personalized Messages

Effective networking begins with making a strong first impression. Whether reaching out on LinkedIn, via email, or through other professional platforms, how you craft your connection request is critical in determining whether your potential contact will accept it. Bland, generic messages often go unnoticed, while a thoughtful, personalized approach can open the door to meaningful relationships. Enter Artificial Intelligence (AI)—a game changer in personalization.

AI tools are helping professionals take the guesswork out of crafting impactful connection requests. AI can suggest tailored content that resonates with your recipient by analyzing individual profiles, interests, and industry trends. When used effectively, these tools increase acceptance rates and lay the foundation for building authentic relationships. However, as with any AI-powered solution, there's a fine line between leveraging technology for efficiency and ensuring human authenticity remains intact.

This chapter explores how AI can transform connection requests through personalization, offering insights into its applications, benefits, challenges, and strategies for maintaining genuine communication.

The Role of AI in Personalized Messaging

AI thrives on data. With access to professional profiles, activity streams, and social media content, AI-powered tools can analyze an individual's public persona to create suggestions for personalized communication. Gone are the days of sending one-size-fits-all messages; instead, AI enables you to engage with contacts on a much deeper, more meaningful level.

Key AI Applications in Personalized Messaging

Here's how AI tools are shaping the landscape of connection requests:

1. Profile Analysis

AI tools scan profiles on platforms like LinkedIn to gain insights into your prospective connection's professional background, skills, interests, and achievements.

- **Example:** Tools like Crystal Knows to analyze how people communicate and recommend language or tone adjustments tailored to an individual's personality type.

2. Content Suggestions

Based on the information it gathers, AI can suggest topics to include in your message, such as referencing shared interests, recent achievements they've highlighted, or mutual connections.

- **Example:** LinkedHelper analyzes LinkedIn profiles to generate personalized opening sentences, such as congratulating a person on a recent job promotion or referencing a book they've written.

3. Templates with a Personal Touch

AI tools create customized templates for outreach that can be quickly adjusted for multiple contacts while retaining individuality.

- **Example:** Sales automation tools like Reply.io incorporate AI to generate tailored connection requests for each recipient based on their professional details and your shared touchpoints.

4. Social Listening and Trend Tracking

AI-powered social listening tools analyze trends and conversations your potential connection engages in. This allows you to reference timely and relevant topics in your outreach.

- **Example:** Tools like Hootsuite Insights can reveal the topics generating buzz within your contact's network, giving you an opportunity to relate directly to their current interests.

5. Behavioral Insights

AI can predict which type of messages will likely resonate based on patterns in the potential connection's activity. For instance, a recipient may respond better to concise requests or those highlighting mutual networking goals.

Benefits of AI-Powered Personalization

Leveraging AI to craft connection requests offers several advantages that can help professionals network smarter and build lasting relationships:

1. Improved Acceptance Rates

Personalized messages stand out in a sea of generic requests. When recipients see that you've taken the time to tailor your outreach, they are far more likely to accept and engage.

2. Time Efficiency

AI dramatically reduces the time spent researching and drafting connection requests. What might take hours of manual research can now be done in seconds, allowing you to reach more contacts without sacrificing personalization.

3. Deeper Engagement

AI helps you establish an immediate connection by referencing relevant details, such as shared experiences, mutual contacts, or recent accomplishments. This sets the stage for a more collaborative and productive networking relationship.

4. Scalability with Precision

For professionals and businesses looking to connect with many prospects, AI ensures that outreach remains personalized and relevant even at scale.

5. Enhanced Learning

AI tools often include analytics features that track responses and engagement rates. You can refine your approach for even better results by analyzing what works and what doesn't.

Challenges in AI-Personalized Messaging

While AI provides powerful advantages, its use in personalizing connection requests isn't without challenges. Understanding these limitations is vital to ensure your outreach feels genuine and ethically sound.

1. Maintaining Authenticity

AI-generated messages can sometimes lack the warmth or subtle nuances that come from human intuition. Over-automating your outreach could make it seem robotic or insincere.

2. Risk of Over-Reliance

While AI can assist in creating compelling messages, it's not a substitute for human effort. Fully relying on AI may lead to a "set it and forget it" mentality, where meaningful engagement takes a back seat.

3. Generic Overtones

When used improperly, AI tools can produce messages that feel templated or overly formulaic, defeating the purpose of personalization.

4. Data Privacy Considerations

AI tools rely on publicly available data to craft personalized messages. While this is often within ethical boundaries, users should be mindful of privacy concerns and avoid anything perceived as intrusive.

5. Balancing Speed and Depth

AI's ability to rapidly generate insights tempts users to prioritize quantity over quality in their outreach, leading to weaker connections.

Tips for Effectively Using AI to Personalize Connection Requests

To take full advantage of AI's personalization capabilities while ensuring your outreach remains authentic and effective, follow these best practices:

1. Start with Clear Objectives

Before crafting your message, be clear on why you're reaching out. Whether to explore collaboration, share insights, or seek mentorship, a clear purpose shapes your outreach and makes it more meaningful.

2. Use AI for Research, Add a Human Touch

Allow AI to gather data and suggest ideas, but don't rely on it to write your entire message. Always add your own voice, perspective, and intent to keep it genuine.

3. Reference Specific Details

AI excels at surfacing relevant details. Use these to your advantage by referencing something unique about the recipient, such as their recent project, a shared interest, or a mutual connection.

4. Keep It Concise and Purposeful

AI might suggest multiple angles for personalization but avoid overwhelming the recipient with too much information. Craft a message that is both easy to read and direct.

5. Test and Optimize

Regularly review the effectiveness of your connection requests. Use analytics from AI tools to identify what resonates most with your audience and adjust your strategy accordingly.

6. Stay Transparent

Be open about how you came across the recipient's information if asked. Transparency builds trust and shows that your outreach is genuine, even if AI provided some groundwork.

7. Respect Boundaries

While AI can uncover a wealth of data, ensure your messages don't cross professional boundaries by including overly personal or intrusive details.

8. Invest in the Follow-Up

Personalized connection requests are only the beginning. Once the connection is made, ensure that your follow-up interactions maintain the same level of authenticity and relevance.

9. Stay Up-to-Date with AI Tools

The AI landscape is constantly evolving. Stay informed about the latest tools and features to leverage cutting-edge capabilities.

In Conclusion

AI has revolutionized how professionals approach networking, making crafting personalized, compelling connection requests more straightforward. By combining data-driven insights with your unique human touch, AI enables you to connect meaningfully and efficiently with the people who matter most to your goals.

The key to success lies in balance. Use AI as a support system—not a substitute—for building relationships. Remember, people value sincerity and effort, even in an AI-driven world. By thoughtfully integrating AI into your outreach strategy, you can expand your network, strengthen connections, and build a professional presence rooted in genuine engagement and meaningful collaboration.

Building Stronger Relationships Through AI-Powered Follow-Ups

When it comes to relationships—whether personal or professional—follow-ups are often the glue that holds connections together. A well-timed, thoughtful follow-up reminds others of your interest, stre543

23ngthens rapport, and demonstrates reliability. Yet despite their importance, follow-ups are often neglected, either because people forget, hesitate, or lack the time to craft meaningful messages.

This is where Artificial Intelligence (AI) is a game changer. AI-powered tools are transforming how we approach follow-ups by automating reminders, personalizing communication, and even providing analytics to optimize timing and content. These innovative technologies ensure that follow-ups happen consistently, efficiently, and in a way that deepens relationships rather than feeling perfunctory.

This book explores how AI can revolutionize your follow-up approach, highlighting its applications, benefits, challenges, and strategies to maintain authenticity while leveraging its capabilities.

The Role of AI in Follow-Ups

AI leverages advanced machine learning, predictive analytics, and natural language processing to make follow-ups more efficient and impactful. AI tools simplify the process by analyzing data and automating repetitive tasks, ensuring you never miss an opportunity to reconnect with contacts or nurture relationships.

Key AI Applications for Follow-Up Strategies

Here's how AI tools are transforming follow-ups into a more strategic and relationship-focused endeavor:

1. Automated Reminders

AI tools help you manage follow-ups by automatically scheduling reminders based on past interactions or pre-configured timelines.

- **Example:** Customer Relationship Management (CRM) platforms like HubSpot automatically notify you when it's time to follow up with a lead or client, ensuring no opportunity slips through the cracks.

2. Personalized Follow-Ups

AI analyzes past interactions, preferences, and behavior to craft follow-up messages that feel tailored and relevant to the recipient.

- **Example:** Tools like Salesforce Einstein or Mailchimp use AI to suggest personalized subject lines and email content based on recipient engagement history.

3. Optimizing Timing

AI tracks previous response patterns and engagement data to determine the best time to send your follow-up.

- **Example:** Platforms like Boomerang for Gmail use AI to analyze email open rates and suggest optimal times for sending follow-ups to increase the likelihood of a response.

4. Natural Language Processing (NLP)

AI can craft professionally worded messages that sound natural and engaging, helping you avoid overly formal or robotic tones while maintaining professionalism.

- **Example:** ChatGPT models integrated into outreach platforms can suggest friendly, conversational follow-up messages that align with your tone.

5. Engagement Analysis

By measuring metrics like click-through rates or response times, AI provides valuable insights into what's working in your follow-ups and what isn't, enabling constant improvements.

- **Example:** Tools like Mixmax and Outreach monitor recipient behavior to help you refine your approach.

6. Behavior Predictions

AI can predict the likelihood of a follow-up's success by analyzing behavioral data, such as past responses or expressed interests, giving you an edge in tailoring your communication.

- **Example:** Predictive lead scoring tools in platforms like Zendesk provide insights into which follow-ups are worth prioritizing.

Benefits of AI-Powered Follow-Ups

By automating and optimizing follow-up communications, AI provides a range of benefits that make strengthening relationships easier and more effective:

1. Improved Efficiency

AI handles much of the heavy lifting, from reminders to crafting initial drafts, saving you hours of effort while maintaining consistency in your outreach.

2. Enhanced Personalization

AI enables you to send follow-ups that resonate personally by drawing on past interactions, shared interests, and recipient preferences.

3. Stronger Relationship Management

By ensuring timely and thoughtful follow-ups, AI helps you maintain strong connections with key stakeholders, clients, or friends, demonstrating your dependability and commitment.

4. Data-Driven Insights

The analytics capabilities of AI tools empower you to measure the impact of your follow-ups, providing a clearer picture of which strategies yield the best results.

5. Scalable Outreach

AI allows you to manage follow-ups at scale without sacrificing personalization. Whether reaching 10 people or 100, AI ensures each message feels tailored and meaningful.

6. Better Timing

By analyzing engagement patterns, AI ensures that follow-ups reach recipients at the right moment, increasing response rates and fostering stronger connections.

Challenges in AI-Powered Follow-Ups

While AI offers undeniable advantages, it's important to recognize and address the challenges that come with incorporating it into your follow-up strategy:

1. Maintaining Authenticity

AI-generated follow-ups can sometimes lack authentic human expression's warmth and emotional depth.

2. Over-reliance on Automation

Entrusting too much of your follow-up process to AI can lead to robotic interactions or a lack of genuine commitment to the relationship.

3. Privacy Concerns

AI tools often rely on data from emails, social profiles, and other online activity, raising potential ethical issues around data privacy.

4. Generic Communication Risks

When not carefully managed, AI-generated messages can feel templated or formulaic, eroding the personal connection you're trying to build.

5. Misaligned Tone or Voice

AI tools may struggle to replicate your unique tone or voice, potentially creating follow-ups that don't align with your personal style or brand.

Tips for Using AI to Enhance Follow-Ups

To effectively incorporate AI while preserving the personal touch of your follow-ups, consider these strategies:

1. Combine AI with Personal Insight

Use AI tools for research and message drafting, but always add your own personal touches. Include anecdotes, shared experiences, or references that AI might miss.

2. Know Your Audience

Ensure that the data AI tools rely on is accurate and up-to-date. A well-tailored follow-up begins with understanding the recipient's needs, status, or preferences.

3. Review AI-Generated Content

Never send follow-ups without reviewing them first. Adjust tone, language, or content to reflect your unique voice.

4. Use Customization Appropriately

Avoid over-customizing to the point where your message feels contrived. Simplicity and sincerity are often more effective than overly detailed personalization.

5. Track and Adjust

Leverage AI-powered analytics to understand how your follow-ups are perceived and refine your approach over time.

6. Be Transparent

If applicable, be upfront about using AI tools in your communication process. Acknowledging this can convey a commitment to efficiency and professionalism without diminishing authenticity.

7. Prioritize Ethics

Respect data privacy regulations by using only publicly available information and practicing ethical standards in using AI tools.

8. Balance Speed with Depth

AI tools can help you scale efforts, but meaningful relationships require time and care. Prioritize depth over frequency in your follow-ups whenever possible.

9. Know When to Go Manual

For particularly important or sensitive relationships, manually crafting a follow-up may be more effective than relying on AI tools.

In Conclusion

AI has opened up new possibilities for enhancing follow-ups, making them smarter, faster, and more impactful. By automating routine tasks and providing valuable insights, AI ensures that no connection remains neglected and every interaction counts.

However, while AI-powered follow-ups offer unmatched efficiency, their effectiveness depends on how thoughtfully they integrate into your relationship-building efforts. Balancing AI's capabilities with the human touch is essential for maintaining authenticity and deepening connections.

By combining AI's precision with genuine intent and effort, you can strengthen your professional and personal relationships, one meaningful follow-up at a time.

Finding Hidden Networking Opportunities with Predictive Analytics

Networking often involves uncovering untapped connections, partnerships, or opportunities others may overlook. Traditionally, this skill has been honed through intuition, experience, and extensive effort. However, predictive analytics has elevated the process to an entirely new level. Predictive analytics combines data, algorithms, and machine learning to analyze historical trends and forecast future opportunities with remarkable precision. For professionals and businesses, this means gaining a strategic advantage in identifying hidden prospects for growth and collaboration.

This subchapter explores how predictive analytics reshapes networking dynamics, highlighting real-world applications, benefits, challenges, and actionable tips to integrate this cutting-edge technology into your networking toolkit.

What is Predictive Analytics?

At its core, predictive analytics uses statistical models and machine learning to analyze past behaviors, patterns, and trends. It creates data-driven forecasts about potential outcomes, guiding users toward more strategic decisions. For networking, this means identifying potential connections, partnerships, and opportunities before they become apparent through traditional methods.

By processing vast amounts of data from sources such as professional platforms, market reports, and social media, predictive analytics enables users to spot patterns and make informed predictions about where and with whom to focus their efforts.

How Predictive Analytics Unearths Networking Opportunities

Predictive analytics isn't just about crunching numbers—it's about revealing connections and insights that might otherwise remain hidden. Here's how it works in practice:

1. Identifying High-Value Connections

Predictive analytics can evaluate existing networks to pinpoint individuals or organizations likely to bring valuable opportunities.

- **Example:** A sales professional can use predictive tools like LinkedIn Talent Insights to identify rising industry leaders or potential collaborators based on shared connections, interests, and engagement levels.

2. Spotting Emerging Market Trends

Predictive analytics can uncover industries, niches, or geographical regions poised for growth by analyzing market data and social sentiment. This allows professionals to align their networking efforts strategically.

- **Example:** A tech entrepreneur might use tools like Tableau or Power BI to analyze regional investments and identify venture capitalists interested in emerging technologies.

3. Uncovering Mutual Interests

Predictive analytics identifies shared interests or mutual goals among contacts to suggest potential synergies.

- **Example:** A marketing manager could use predictive lead-scoring tools to find potential partners for collaborative campaigns based on historical data from past collaborations.

4. Tracking Behavioral Patterns

Predictive analytics analyzes analytics and can determine when individuals or companies are interphase or researching specific topics by analyzing online behavior, such as likes, shares, or content downloads.

- **Example:** Companies like Bombora monitor intent data to notify businesses when potential partners are signaling interest in their services or industry.

5. Forecasting Networking Gaps

Predictive models can highlight weak spots in an individual's or organization's network and suggest areas for expansion to increase influence and reach.

- **Example:** A business consultant could use predictive analytics to identify underrepresented sectors within their network and proactively target professionals or organizations in those areas.

Real-world applications of Predictive Analytics in Networking

Businesses and individuals across industries are harnessing the power of predictive analytics to enhance their networking strategies. Below are some tangible examples:

- **Business Partnerships:** A SaaS company uses data-driven insights to identify other companies whose services complement their own, leading to mutual partnerships that enhance product offerings.
- **Recruitment:** HR professionals apply predictive models to find candidates who align with their company culture and long-term goals, improving retention rates and team cohesion.
- **Content Collaboration:** Influencers and thought leaders use predictive tools on platforms like BuzzSumo to find complementary creators or brands for joint campaigns.
- **Sales and Client Acquisition:** Sales teams utilize platforms like Salesforce Einstein to anticipate which prospects will most likely convert into clients, optimizing outreach strategies.
- **Event Networking:** Event organizers use predictive analytics to recommend attendees who align with each other's goals, fostering more successful networking opportunities during conferences.

Benefits of Predictive Analytics in Networking

Integrating predictive analytics into networking strategies opens doors to numerous advantages, helping professionals stay ahead of the curve.

1. Enhanced Foresight

Predictive analytics enables users to identify opportunities before competitors, offering a definitive strategic edge.

- **Example:** A small consulting firm foresees a demand spike for sustainability initiatives by analyzing emerging government policies, allowing it to proactively reach out to companies needing such expertise.

2. Strategic Targeting

By refining focus areas, predictive analytics ensures networking efforts are directed toward the most promising opportunities, maximizing ROI.

3. Broader Reach

Predictive tools help individuals and businesses connect outside their immediate networks, expanding access to new industries, geographical regions, or niche markets.

4. Data-Driven Decisions

Unlike intuition-based approaches, predictive analytics delivers objective insights grounded in data. This reduces risk and increases the accuracy of targeting decisions.

5. Improved Relationship Building

Identifying mutual goals and strategic synergies paves the way for stronger, more collaborative relationships.

Challenges in Using Predictive Analytics for Networking

While predictive analytics offers powerful advantages, it's accompanied by caveats that must be managed to ensure success.

1. Data Accuracy

The quality of predictions depends entirely on the quality of the data being analyzed. Outdated, incomplete, or biased datasets can result in flawed insights.

2. Over-Reliance on Technology

Predictive analytics is a tool, not a solution. Over-relying on predictive models removes the human intuition and creativity that are crucial for meaningful interactions.

3. Privacy Concerns

Analyzing online behavior, preferences, and demographics raises ethical questions about data usage. Using predictive analytics responsibly and transparently is essential to maintain trust.

4. Emerging Trend Overwhelm

The sheer volume of opportunities highlighted by predictive tools can be overwhelming, making it difficult to prioritize effectively.

5. Limited Intangibles

Predictive models cannot account for "gut instincts" or unquantifiable factors such as emotional intelligence and rapport, which often define successful networking endeavors.

Strategies for Effectively Using Predictive Analytics in Networking

To make the most of predictive analytics while overcoming potential challenges, consider these actionable tips:

1. Validate Data Sources

Ensure the data-feeding predictive models are accurate, up-to-date, and ethically obtained. Reliable data leads to more precise predictions.

2. Define Your Goals

Be clear about what you want to achieve through networking—identifying new clients, forming strategic partnerships, or exploring a market niche. Tailor your use of predictive analytics to align with these goals.

3. Use Tools Wisely

Leverage specialized tools for specific networking purposes. For instance, LinkedIn Sales Navigator can be used for professional connections and as a social listening tool to uncover influencers or market trends.

4. Don't Neglect the Human Element

Strike a balance between predictive insights and personal judgment. Relationships thrive on authenticity and emotional connection, so complement data-driven strategies with meaningful, in-person engagement.

5. Start Small and Scale

Implement predictive analytics in a single area, such as targeting key prospects. Once you're comfortable with the results, expand its use to other aspects of your networking strategy.

6. Monitor and Adjust

Continuously track the accuracy and effectiveness of your predictive models. Use feedback to refine algorithms, ensuring that insights remain relevant and actionable over time.

In Conclusion

Predictive analytics offers a revolutionary way to uncover hidden networking opportunities. It allows professionals to connect with the right people, anticipate trends, and strategically grow their networks. However, technology should be seen as an assistant, not a replacement for human effort and intuition.

By integrating predictive analytics thoughtfully and responsibly, you can identify opportunities that would otherwise remain invisible—giving you the foresight and strategic advantage to thrive in an increasingly competitive landscape. Networking isn't just about who you know; it's about who you're about to meet—and predictive analytics can guide you to the right doors to knock on.

Bonus
Download

SCAN ME

Chapter 5

Content Creation Made Easy with AI

Creating engaging, high-quality content is vital in today's marketing landscape. It's what captures attention, cultivates connections, and drives decisions. However, crafting effective content can often be time-consuming and resource-intensive, especially with the growing demand for diverse formats, rapid turnaround times, and tailored messaging. Fortunately, artificial intelligence (AI) has stepped in as a powerful ally, revolutionizing how marketers and creators approach the content creation process.

AI is no longer just a futuristic concept—it has become an essential tool, streamlining content generation while pushing the boundaries of what's possible. With its ability to analyze vast amounts of data, understand user behavior, and assist in creative processes, AI simplifies producing text, images, videos, and other engaging materials. By doing so, it not only saves time but also inspires fresh ideas and ensures content resonates with target audiences across platforms.

AI's Versatility in Content Creation

AI's impact on content creation extends across multiple mediums, empowering marketers to craft materials for every corner of the digital world. Here's a glimpse of what it can do:

- **Text Generation:** AI-enabled tools can write compelling copy in seconds, from blog posts to social media captions. Using natural language processing (NLP) techniques, these tools generate coherent, relevant text tailored to audience preferences.

Additionally, AI refines text through editing and optimization, ensuring SEO-friendly and impactful content.

- **Image Creation and Optimization:** Visual content is a marketing staple, and AI tools now help design, edit, and enhance images to fit branding needs. Whether creating custom illustrations, selecting the perfect color palettes, or resizing graphics for various platforms, AI handles it with precision.

- **Video Production:** AI has also revolutionized video content, a medium with unmatched engagement potential. AI tools automate processes from scripting to editing, making video creation accessible even for small teams or solo creators. AI can also tailor video elements, such as subtitles or voiceovers, ensuring inclusivity and personalization.

Benefits of AI in Content Creation

Integrating AI into content strategies offers a range of benefits that make it an invaluable resource for marketers and creators alike:

1. **Enhanced Productivity:** AI takes care of repetitive tasks like drafting, formatting, and keywording, freeing up time for you to focus on strategy and originality.

2. **Personalization at Scale:** With AI, crafting content tailored to specific audiences becomes simpler. AI algorithms analyze user behavior and preferences to develop messaging that truly resonates.

3. **Creative Inspiration:** AI tools can suggest topics, ideas, and approaches based on the latest trends and data, sparking creativity and helping you explore new content directions.

4. **Cost and Time Efficiency:** AI reduces the time and expenses traditionally required for content production by streamlining processes and offering automated solutions.

5. **Optimized for Platforms:** AI ensures your content performs well on different channels by adapting its structure, tone, and format for specific platforms like social media, blogs, or video-sharing sites.

Navigating Challenges with AI

While AI offers incredible advantages, it also comes with challenges that demand thoughtful consideration:

- **Maintaining Originality:** Because AI often relies on pre-existing data, ensuring your content stands out and avoids repetition requires diligent review and revision.

- **Avoiding Over-Reliance:** AI should complement human creativity, not replace it. Striking the right balance ensures that content remains personal, authentic, and relatable.

- **Ethical Considerations:** Responsible use of AI is essential to avoid issues like copyright infringement or data misuse. Transparency and ethical practices should guide every step of the process.

Setting the Stage

Chapter 5 will explore the growing role of AI in content creation. It will explore specific applications, from writing to video editing, and provide actionable insights on how to use these tools to their fullest potential. You'll learn how AI can transform how you conceptualize, produce, and deliver content, enabling you to stay ahead in a competitive marketplace.

By the end of this chapter, you'll clearly understand how AI tools can be more than just a convenience—they can be the key to unlocking efficiency, creativity, and success in the evolving art of content marketing. Whether you're a seasoned professional or just beginning to integrate AI into your workflow, the insights ahead will help you harness the power of AI to make content creation easier and more impactful.

Generating Engaging Posts Using AI Writing Tools

Creating content that truly connects with your audience is both a science and an art. Whether you're crafting the perfect Instagram caption, a thought-provoking blog entry, or an educational LinkedIn post, your ability to engage readers hinges on how well you balance creativity, relevance, and strategy. This balancing act has become significantly more manageable thanks to the rise of AI writing tools. These powerful technologies are transforming content creation by providing marketers, writers, and businesses the means to create compelling posts faster, smarter, and more effectively.

This book explores how AI writing tools empower creators to generate engaging content for social media, blogs, and beyond. We'll examine their features, benefits, and challenges and share actionable tips to help you maximize their potential.

What Are AI Writing Tools?

AI writing tools are software applications powered by artificial intelligence. They generate or refine text based on prompts, user instructions, and pre-analyzed data. By leveraging advanced techniques like natural language processing (NLP) and machine learning, these tools can churn out captivating phrases, cohesive paragraphs, and even entire books in minutes.

Unlike traditional automation, AI tools don't just repeat pre-programmed scripts; they draw upon vast datasets and algorithms to create context-aware, personalized, and optimized content for specific platforms. From brainstorming ideas to structuring paragraphs, these tools act as robust assistants at every stage of the content creation process.

Key Features of AI Writing Tools

Modern AI writing tools have features designed to simplify and supercharge content creation. Here's how they help you craft engaging posts:

1. Content Suggestions

AI tools can suggest ideas and headlines, eliminating writer's block. Platforms like Jasper or Writesonic prompt fresh, data-driven ideas by analyzing popular trends within your niche.

2. Tone Adjustments

Whether you're aiming for a professional LinkedIn update or a fun Twitter thread, tone matters. Tools like Grammarly and Jasper allow users to adjust the tone of their content to suit their audience or platform.

3. SEO Optimization

Search engine visibility is crucial for blogs and online books. Tools such as Surfer SEO and Clearscope recommend keyword placements, headings, and readability improvements to boost ranking potential.

4. Content Structuring

AI can generate outlines or complete drafts, organizing your thoughts logically and cohesively. For example, apps like ChatGPT can build frameworks for blog posts from scratch based on pre-specified themes.

5. Personalization

AI tools like Persado can craft messages tailored to specific demographics or user segments by analyzing audience behavior and preferences.

6. Editing and Proofreading

Beyond creation, AI can refine your text to improve clarity, grammar, and effectiveness. Tools like Grammarly suggest revisions to ensure polished, professional final drafts.

7. Multilingual Capabilities

AI writing tools like DeepL Write and Writesonic allow users to generate or translate posts in multiple languages, ensuring global accessibility and reach.

Popular AI Writing Tools to Consider

If you're excited about incorporating AI into your content strategy, here are some platforms worth exploring:

- **Jasper:** Offers a comprehensive suite for creating engaging blog content, social media posts, and email campaigns with adjustable tone and style options.
- **Writesonic:** Known for crafting compelling ads, landing pages, and product descriptions using AI-based text generation.
- **Grammarly:** Refines text with grammar and tone suggestions, making it a go-to for editing and content clarity.

- **Surfer SEO:** Delivers SEO insights to help creators craft blogs optimized for search engines.
- **ChatGPT:** Generates well-rounded books, discussions, and scripts using conversational AI.
- **Copy.ai:** Focused on marketing, this tool provides high-quality, engaging copy for ads, social platforms, and more.

Benefits of AI Writing Tools

The increasing adoption of AI in content creation stems from its numerous advantages. Here are the key benefits that make these tools indispensable:

1. Time-Saving Efficiency

AI tools streamline content creation by handling repetitive tasks like brainstorming, editing, and keyword insertion. This allows creators to produce high-quality posts more quickly and focus on strategy.

2. Creativity Enhancement

AI tools can effortlessly generate new ideas, suggesting angles, headlines, and anecdotes. They serve as creative partners, helping you refine your concepts and add diverse perspectives to your work.

3. Audience Personalization

AI-driven insights help you craft posts tailored to specific user segments. Personalized content resonates better with readers and drives higher engagement.

4. Improved Quality and Accuracy

With built-in editing features, AI tools ensure your content is free of grammar mistakes, typos, and awkward phrasings.

5. Consistency Across Platforms

AI allows you to create content that fits the unique requirements of each social or publishing platform, from character limits to optimal formats.

6. Leveling the Playing Field

For individuals and businesses without large marketing budgets, AI tools offer affordable solutions for creating professional-grade content.

Challenges in Using AI Writing Tools

Despite their many advantages, AI writing tools have certain limitations that creators should consider.

1. Generic Outputs

AI tools often rely on existing datasets, which may lead to repetitive or uninspired outputs. Personalization and fine-tuning are necessary to make your content unique.

2. Context Understanding

AI lacks deep comprehension and may generate off-target or tone-deaf content in specific contexts.

3. Authenticity Concerns

The overuse of AI-generated text can make written voices feel robotic or lack the warmth and emotion of human storytelling.

4. Ethical Considerations

Issues such as unintentional copyright violations and data misuse are valid concerns when using AI for content creation.

5. Limited Intuition

AI can handle data and patterns—but it can't replace human instincts, creativity, or deep cultural understanding in crafting content that truly stands out.

Tips for Generating Engaging Content with AI

To overcome these challenges and make the most of AI for your posts, consider these practical strategies:

1. Review and Revise

Never rely solely on AI-generated text. Always review, tweak, and refine the output to align with your brand's voice, messaging, and values.

2. Use Prompts Strategically

Be clear and specific in your prompts to guide AI tools toward outputs that match your vision. The better the input, the stronger the output.

3. Combine AI with Human Touch

Focus on creating a truly engaging narrative by infusing AI outputs with emotion, storytelling, and originality.

4. Experiment Purposefully

Test AI features—such as tone adjustments or content templates—on different platforms to determine what works best for your audience.

5. Stay Ethical and Transparent

Disclose the use of AI in creating sponsored or branded content, and ensure your posts avoid plagiarism or information misuse.

6. Use AI for Inspiration, Not Dictation

Leverage AI to spark ideas, generate outlines, or identify keywords—then bring it all to life with your unique perspective.

In Conclusion

AI writing tools are invaluable companions for content creators who want to work smarter, not harder. These tools unlock new levels of efficiency and creativity by automating tedious tasks, sparking creativity, and optimizing content for platforms. However, the most engaging posts aren't born from algorithms alone. The blend of AI precision with human emotion, authenticity, and strategy creates content that truly resonates.

Harness the power of AI writing tools to generate posts that captivate, inspire, and convert, but always infuse your unique voice to craft narratives that leave a lasting impression. When used thoughtfully, AI can amplify your creative potential and cement your voice in the crowded digital arena.

AI Analysis of Trending Topics for Maximum Visibility

Staying relevant in a fast-paced digital world is no small feat. Whether you're a content creator, marketer, or brand strategist, keeping up with trending topics is key to capturing attention and engaging your audience. However, relying solely on manual research to identify emerging trends can be time-intensive and inefficient. This is where artificial intelligence (AI) becomes a game-changer. AI tools are transforming how we analyze trending topics, equipping creators with powerful insights to craft timely, impactful content that maximizes visibility and engagement.

This book explores how AI-driven trend analysis works, explores its applications, and offers practical tips for using AI to supercharge your content strategies.

The Mechanics of AI in Trend Analysis

AI tools for trend analysis use advanced algorithms and machine learning models to monitor, predict, and assess shifts in online behavior, sentiment, and interest. AI can uncover patterns that indicate trending topics by processing vast amounts of data from social media platforms, search engines, news outlets, and forums like Reddit.

For instance, natural language processing (NLP) tools can parse millions of social media posts to detect which keywords, hashtags, or phrases are on the rise. Combining these insights with predictive analytics, AI can even forecast future trends—giving marketers a leg up in creating content ahead of the curve.

Workflow of AI Trend Analysis

1. **Data Collection:** AI gathers information from multiple data streams, including social platforms like Twitter, search engines (e.g., Google Trends), and real-time newsfeeds.
2. **Pattern Recognition:** AI uses algorithms to detect correlations between content engagement, keywords, and user behaviors to identify "topics on the rise."
3. **Sentiment Analysis:** AI evaluates the tone of conversations around a trend, determining whether its reception is positive, negative, or neutral.
4. **Insights and Recommendations:** Based on its analysis, the AI provides actionable insights—recommending areas of focus, potential keywords, and strategies to capitalize on the trend efficiently.

Applications of AI Trend Analysis

AI-powered tools for analyzing trends are versatile, offering a range of applications that enhance content strategies and marketing campaigns. Below are some of the most common use cases:

1. Tracking Emerging Trends

AI platforms like BuzzSumo and Brandwatch can monitor live industry chatter, surfacing topics gaining traction. For example, if a new health fad dominates social media, a wellness brand can create relevant posts or videos.

2. Predicting Future Topics

AI can analyze the present and predict tomorrow's trends. By examining historical data and user behavior patterns, tools like Google Trends and Exploding Topics can help creators prepare content ahead of time, positioning them as thought leaders.

3. Optimizing Content Strategies

AI tools like HubSpot and Crayon offer trend-based recommendations for content formats, headlines, and distribution channels, ensuring optimized performance. For example, noticing a peak in video content engagement might prompt marketers to focus on short-form videos.

4. Social Sentiment Monitoring

AI monitors the tone of online conversations to gauge public sentiment toward a trend. This insight enables brands to engage in relevant discussions while avoiding controversial topics that could harm their reputation.

5. Localized Trend Analysis

What trends in one region might not resonate elsewhere? AI tools help tailor trend analysis locally or nationally, ensuring content is culturally relevant and localized for maximum appeal.

6. Competitive Analysis

AI tools can also provide intelligence on competitors by examining how rival brands respond to trends. This allows businesses to spot gaps and opportunities to stand out.

Benefits of AI in Trend Analysis

Integrating AI into your trend analysis workflow offers numerous advantages, making it an essential tool for marketers and creators.

1. Enhanced Relevance

AI ensures your content aligns with what your audience cares about—right when they care about it. This connection helps build authenticity, trust, and deeper engagement.

2. Strategic Advantage

By identifying trends faster than competitors and predicting future directions, you can position yourself as a leader in your industry, sparking conversations instead of following them.

3. Time and Cost Efficiency

Manually researching trends can take hours, but AI completes this task within seconds, freeing up time to focus on creating and refining content strategies.

4. Data-Driven Decisions

AI trend analysis eliminates guesswork by using data and metrics to guide strategic decisions, resulting in better outcomes and more apparent ROI.

5. Scalability

With the ability to process enormous datasets, AI tools scale across industries, languages, and demographics, ensuring creators can track trends globally and locally.

Challenges in AI-Driven Trend Analysis

Despite its many benefits, AI trend analysis has limitations that should be approached with caution.

1. Data Accuracy

AI tools are only as reliable as the data they process. Biased or incomplete datasets can lead to inaccurate predictions or missed opportunities.

2. Over-reliance on Algorithms

While AI excels at identifying patterns, it lacks the creativity and intuition humans bring to storytelling. Solely relying on AI might result in generic or uninspired content.

3. Navigating Noise

The internet is brimming with fleeting fads and misinformation. AI occasionally highlights short-lived or controversial trends, requiring manual verification to ensure relevance.

4. Adapting to Audience Nuances

AI often struggles to understand the emotional and cultural subtleties that make certain trends resonate, where human insight becomes critical.

Tips for Using AI in Trend Analysis

Here are actionable strategies for leveraging AI tools to analyze trending topics effectively:

1. Choose the Right Tools

Explore AI platforms tailored to your industry and goals. From social listening tools like Brandwatch to SEO platforms like SEMrush, select tools that align with your content needs.

2. Verify Data Manually

Augment AI insights with your own research. Cross-check trends to ensure their relevance and longevity before incorporating them into your content strategy.

3. Don't Chase Every Trend

Focus on trends that align with your brand values and audience interests. Not every trend is worth pursuing; jumping on the wrong ones can dilute your credibility.

4. Combine AI with Human Creativity

Use AI to spark ideas and locate opportunities, but infuse the final execution with human storytelling, emotion, and originality to make it impactful.

5. Focus on Localization

For global businesses, prioritize localized trend analysis to ensure the content resonates with diverse audiences across different regions.

6. Adapt Quickly

Once a relevant trend is identified, respond promptly. The faster you can create content around it, the more likely you will capture attention during its peak.

In Conclusion

AI has revolutionized how we analyze trending topics, offering creators and marketers a competitive edge to stay visible, relevant, and timely. While AI tools have exceptional abilities to monitor, predict, and optimize trends, their full potential is unlocked when used alongside human intuition and strategy.

By harnessing AI's capabilities and blending them with creative storytelling, you can craft content that not only rides the wave of relevance but also sparks meaningful engagement. Trends move fast, but with AI, so can you.

Leveraging AI to Create Engaging Visuals and Infographics

Visual content is a powerful force in today's digital era. From eye-catching infographics to striking social media posts, visuals capture attention, communicate ideas, and leave lasting impressions. However, creating visually appealing and effective graphics can be daunting, requiring technical skills, design knowledge, and time investment. Enter artificial intelligence (AI) – the modern solution revolutionizing how visuals and infographics are created.

AI-powered tools simplify the design process, automate complex tasks, and spark creativity, making it easier than ever to produce high-quality visuals. This book explores how AI is transforming visual content creation, the benefits it offers, and practical tips to unlock its potential.

How AI is Transforming Visual Content Creation

AI tools are changing the game in visual content design by leveraging techniques like machine learning, computer vision, and natural language processing (NLP). These technologies enable AI to analyze design trends, predict audience preferences, and automate tedious design tasks such as layout alignment, color selection, and resizing.

Key Capabilities of AI in Visual Design

1. **Automated Design Suggestions**

   AI tools like Canva and Designhill can analyze a user's text input or desired theme to automatically generate suggested layouts, making the design process faster and less intimidating for beginners.

2. **Color Palette Generation**

   AI platforms like Coolors and Adobe Color use algorithms to generate harmonious color palettes. They can suggest colors based on user preferences or images, ensuring visually appealing combinations.

3. **Typography Optimization**

   AI can recommend font pairings that enhance readability and aesthetic appeal, streamlining an otherwise complex decision-making process.

4. **Layout Optimization**

   AI tools like Visme analyze the content and automatically adjust layouts to create visually balanced and well-structured designs.

5. **Smart Resizing for Multi-Platform Use**

   AI simplifies creating content for multiple platforms by automatically resizing designs to fit different formats, such as Instagram posts, Facebook ads, or YouTube covers.

6. **Stock Image and Icon Recommendations**

   Platforms like Shutterstock and Adobe Stock harness AI to suggest relevant images and icons based on user input, reducing the time spent searching for resources.

7. **Data to Infographics Conversion**

AI-powered tools like Infogram and Piktochart convert raw data into attractive, easy-to-understand infographics, making data storytelling accessible for all.

Popular AI Tools for Visual Design

If you're ready to explore AI-driven visual content creation, here are some leading tools to consider:

- **Canva**
  Canva uses AI to generate design templates, suggest color schemes, and customize layouts, offering an intuitive platform suitable for designers of any skill level.

- **Piktochart**
  Ideal for infographics, Piktochart turns data into compelling visuals through its AI-powered chart and graph suggestions.

- **Adobe Express**
  Adobe's AI-powered tool provides quick design templates and custom options for everything from social posts to presentations.

- **Visme**
  Visme specializes in branding and business materials, delivering AI-driven recommendations for layouts, icons, and audience-specific designs.

- **Crello**
  Crello (now VistaCreate) uses AI to generate professional-quality visuals optimized for specific formats, such as animated social media posts.

- **Khroma**
  A niche AI tool focusing on colors, Khroma suggests color palettes based on personal preferences, ensuring designs resonate with brand identity.

Benefits of Using AI for Visuals and Infographics

Adopting AI for visual content creation offers numerous advantages that can enhance your design workflows and overall communication strategy:

1. Time Efficiency

By automating repetitive or technical tasks like resizing, alignment, and font selection, AI significantly reduces the time typically spent on the design process.

2. Cost-Effective Solutions

Hiring professional designers or investing in elaborate design software isn't feasible for everyone. AI tools offer affordable alternatives to produce professional-quality visuals.

3. Elevated Creativity

AI tools inspire creativity by suggesting fresh design ideas, layouts, and color schemes that may not have crossed your mind.

4. Accessible for Beginners

AI-powered platforms deliver user-friendly interfaces and guided suggestions for those with no design background, enabling non-experts to create polished visuals.

5. Customizable and Scalable Designs

AI makes it easy to adapt designs to multiple platforms with a few clicks, helping brands maintain consistency across formats and channels.

6. Enhanced Data Visualization

Infographics are crucial for presenting complex data in a digestible way. AI transforms raw statistics into clear, visually appealing charts and graphs, improving audience comprehension.

7. Real-Time Adjustments

Some AI tools can adapt designs in real time based on new inputs or shifting brand requirements, adding flexibility to the creative process.

Challenges in AI-Driven Design

Despite its many strengths, AI design tools also come with certain limitations:

1. Lack of Originality

AI generates designs based on training data, sometimes leading to generic or overly template-like visuals. Staying unique requires additional human input.

2. Creative Limitations

While AI excels at following patterns, it may struggle with non-traditional or out-of-the-box ideas that deviate from its programming.

3. Quality Assurance

AI-generated visuals may require human oversight to ensure they meet standards of quality, branding, and relevance for specific audiences.

4. Ethical Concerns

Using AI in design raises questions about intellectual property rights and originality, particularly when designs are built on pre-existing datasets.

5. Over-reliance

Depending too heavily on AI tools can sideline human creativity and understate the importance of authentic storytelling in the design process.

Tips for Effectively Leveraging AI in Visual Design

Maximizing the potential of AI in creating visuals and infographics requires thoughtful strategy. Here are some tips to help you get started:

1. Define Your Objectives Clearly

Before using an AI tool, outline your design goals—whether for brand-specific visuals, infographics for presentations, or multi-platform social posts.

2. Start with Templates

AI tools often provide pre-designed templates as a starting point. Choose one that aligns with your vision, then customize it for a unique touch.

3. Refine AI-Generated Outputs

AI-generated designs are a great foundation, but the final touches should be edited and personalized to reflect your brand's personality and message.

4. Blend AI with Human Creativity

Use AI to handle technical tasks while focusing your energy on strategic, creative direction that resonates emotionally with your audience.

5. Test and Iterate

Experiment by generating multiple versions of visuals and analyzing audience responses to determine what works best.

6. Stay Ethical and Transparent

Disclose AI's role in the design process or adjust outputs to ensure originality and ethical compliance.

7. Keep Learning

AI tools constantly evolve, so stay updated on features and capabilities that make your design process more efficient and impactful.

In Conclusion

Integrating AI into visual content creation reshapes how images, infographics, and designs are developed. With its ability to automate workflows, enhance creativity, and optimize content for diverse platforms, AI empowers marketers, creators, and brands to deliver eye-catching visuals that resonate with their audiences.

However, balancing its capabilities with human creativity is the key to harnessing AI's full potential. By using AI tools to augment—not replace—your design process, you can achieve visuals that are engaging and uniquely reflective of your brand.

Whether you're a seasoned design professional or a novice content creator, AI provides endless opportunities to elevate your visual storytelling and make a lasting impact in an increasingly competitive digital world.

Automating Engagement with AI for Timely Responses

Timely and meaningful engagement is the lifeline of successful customer interactions in today's fast-paced digital environment. Whether addressing customer queries, managing social media interactions, or responding to emails, the ability to provide swift and accurate replies can significantly enhance customer experience. However, keeping up with the sheer volume of communications is challenging, especially as businesses grow. This is where Artificial Intelligence (AI) is revolutionizing how customer engagements are managed.

AI-powered tools are designed to automate responses, streamline workflows, and maintain efficiency while preserving the value of businesses' customer-centric approach. This book explores how AI can automate platform engagement, highlights its benefits and challenges, and offers actionable tips to maximize its potential.

How AI is Redefining Engagement

AI's ability to analyze, learn, and execute tasks makes it a powerful asset for automating engagement. Leveraging machine learning (ML), natural language processing (NLP), and predictive analytics, AI can handle customer interactions with minimal supervision. From chatbots offering 24/7 support to personalized email campaigns, AI tools can respond to queries, manage tasks, and even predict customer needs—all in real-time.

AI in Customer Interaction Channels

1. **Chatbots**

    Powered by NLP, AI chatbots like those used by Zendesk and Drift can interpret customer queries in natural language and reply with relevant answers. These bots can handle simple to moderately complex queries, freeing up human agents for higher-level tasks.

2. **Email Automation**

    AI platforms such as Mailchimp and ActiveCampaign analyze recipient behavior (click rates, open rates, etc.) and send timely personalized email responses. They can also segment audiences for targeted engagement.

3. **Social Media Responses**

    Tools like Sprinklr and Hootsuite Insights enable businesses to engage with followers by automatically responding to comments, mentions, or direct messages. These tools prioritize urgent interactions by analyzing sentiment and assigning importance.

4. **Voice Assistants**

   AI-powered virtual assistants, such as Alexa for Business or Google Assistant, provide voice-based real-time responses, enhancing accessibility and customer interaction speed.

5. **Live Chat Support**

   AI integrations in live chat platforms like Intercom allow bots to initiate conversations, escalate issues to human agents, or suggest helpful resources based on customer input.

6. **Feedback Collection**

   AI tools like Qualtrics use automated surveys and sentiment analysis to proactively gather and respond to customer feedback, ensuring timely and relevant follow-ups.

How AI Ensures Timeliness

AI tools process data in milliseconds, enabling lightning-fast responses. Customer inquiries that would take humans minutes or even hours to address are resolved instantly using pre-defined workflows, algorithms, and decision trees. For instance, when a customer reports an issue via live chat, the chatbot can immediately pull up the customer's order history, diagnose the problem, and suggest solutions.

Benefits of AI in Automating Engagement

Automating engagement with AI offers a range of advantages that go beyond just speed. These benefits enhance both operational efficiency and customer satisfaction.

1. Faster Response Times

AI ensures no customer inquiry is left hanging. With automated systems working around the clock, your team can respond faster to every tweet, comment, or email—improving response rates and minimizing delays.

2. Round-the-clock Availability

Unlike human support teams, AI-powered engagement systems operate 24/7, handling requests during off-hours or holidays without breaking stride.

3. Personalized Interactions

AI tools analyze customer profiles, preferences, and past interactions to deliver tailored responses. For example, an AI assistant might recommend products based on the customer's buying history or suggest relevant upgrades.

4. Improved Customer Satisfaction

Timely and effective responses leave customers feeling valued and heard. When engagement is seamless, customer loyalty and trust grow exponentially.

5. Scalability

AI systems can manage tens of thousands of interactions simultaneously—something no human workforce could achieve. This capability makes it a game-changer for growing businesses.

6. Cost Efficiency

Reduced reliance on extensive human customer support teams helps cut costs while maintaining high service standards.

7. Data-Driven Insights

AI engagement tools collect and analyze data to uncover patterns, highlight recurring customer pain points, and recommend strategic adjustments, empowering businesses with actionable feedback.

8. Enhanced Focus for Human Teams

By automating routine tasks, AI allows human representatives to focus on resolving complex or high-value customer queries that require empathy and creativity.

Challenges of Automating Customer Engagement

While AI offers immense opportunities for automating engagement, it also brings its own set of challenges.

1. Lack of Personal Touch

While efficient, AI tools often lack the emotional intelligence required to empathize with customers or solve nuanced problems. Overusing automation may make interactions feel impersonal.

2. Difficulty Handling Complex Queries

AI tools excel with straightforward queries but struggle with complex problems requiring judgment, reasoning, or creative solutions.

3. Risk of Miscommunication

Misinterpreted inquiries or inaccurate responses can frustrate customers and harm the brand's reputation. Language ambiguities or regional nuances may exacerbate such issues.

4. Over-Automation

Over-reliance on AI can alienate customers who prefer human engagement. Striking the right balance is critical.

5. Data Privacy Concerns

Automation requires collecting and processing customer data, which, if mismanaged, could lead to breaches or compliance issues.

Tips for Effectively Automating Engagement

Addressing these challenges while maximizing efficiency is essential to succeeding with AI-powered engagement. Below are tips to help you implement an effective strategy.

1. Use AI as a Support, Not a Substitute

AI works best in partnership with human teams. Automate repetitive or time-sensitive tasks but leave creative and complex queries to human representatives.

2. Prioritize personalization

Leverage AI to tailor engagement based on each customer's preferences, purchase history, and interactions. Personalized messaging feels more authentic and creates stronger connections.

3. Train AI on Brand Voice and Values

Ensure your AI tools understand and replicate your brand's tone, style, and voice. Use FAQ datasets and customer interaction scripts to keep responses consistent yet relatable.

4. Monitor and Fine-Tune Performance

Regularly evaluate AI tools to assess their success rates, spot miscommunications, and refine algorithms for relevance and accuracy.

5. Set Clear Boundaries for AI Usage

Assign specific tasks to AI, such as answering FAQs or redirecting inquiries, and create clear escalation paths for human agents to intervene when needed.

6. Ensure Data Security

Invest in secure AI platforms and comply with data privacy regulations to build customer trust. Encrypt sensitive information or anonymize data where possible.

7. Make AI Interactions Transparent

Disclose the use of AI in customer interactions and provide an easy option for customers to connect with a human agent when necessary.

8. Focus on Continuous Improvement

AI technologies evolve rapidly. Stay informed about new advancements and regularly upgrade your systems to deliver the best possible experience.

In Conclusion

Automating engagement with AI is revolutionizing customer service, making it faster, more accessible, and data-driven. From chatbots and email automation to sentiment analysis on social media, AI tools empower businesses to streamline communication while boosting customer satisfaction.

While challenges like maintaining a personal touch and managing complex queries remain, these can be mitigated by balancing automation with human empathy and ensuring interaction transparency. Ultimately, businesses that effectively leverage AI for timely engagement will enhance customer experiences and establish themselves as innovators in their industries.

By combining the power of AI with thoughtful strategies, you can build a customer service experience that feels both efficient and authentic— meeting today's demands while preparing for tomorrow's opportunities.

Chapter 6
Winning the Algorithm Game

Powerful algorithms rule the digital landscape. These algorithms determine what content is seen, shared, and engaged with across search engines, social media platforms, and even personalized recommendations. These algorithms are the architects of online visibility—they decide which blog posts get prime spots in search results, which videos go viral, and which ads get clicked. For marketers, understanding and mastering these algorithms is the ultimate key to staying competitive and relevant.

Search engine optimization (SEO) is the most well-known arena of the algorithm game. Search giants like Google employ complex algorithms to rank web pages based on relevance, authority, and hundreds of other factors. A firm grasp of SEO techniques can propel a business to the top of search results, driving organic traffic. Social media platforms, on the other hand, operate with entirely different priorities. Algorithms on platforms like Instagram, TikTok, or LinkedIn are designed to maximize engagement by pushing content that resonates most with individual users. Simultaneously, recommendation systems, from Netflix to Amazon, are fine-tuned to deliver hyper-personalized suggestions, making personalization another powerful frontier in the algorithm-driven world.

Navigating this complex and constantly shifting ecosystem is no easy feat. Algorithms change frequently, often with little notice, forcing marketers to adapt their strategies continually. What works today—be it a specific keyword strategy for SEO or a trending content type for social media—might be obsolete tomorrow. This dynamic environment can feel overwhelming as marketers race to understand the rules of engagement, optimize their content, and avoid penalties from misaligned tactics.

But where there's a challenge, there's an opportunity—especially for those who leverage modern tools like artificial intelligence (AI). AI is transforming the way marketers approach these algorithms. With its ability to analyze large datasets, detect patterns, and generate insights at lightning speed, AI is a compass in algorithmic systems' unpredictable waters. For example, AI-powered tools can identify optimal keywords for SEO, predict content trends on social media, and personalize campaigns at scale—all while providing real-time recommendations to stay ahead of algorithm shifts.

However, mastering the algorithm game isn't just about playing by the rules; it's about outsmarting them. Marketers who succeed in this space don't merely follow trends—they innovate, crafting strategies that anticipate algorithm updates and set them apart from competitors. This requires a deep understanding of algorithms, a keen eye for analyzing results, and the ability to adapt quickly.

This chapter dives into the complexities of winning the algorithm game. It explores the mechanics of search engine algorithms, the nuances of social media algorithms, and the potential of AI to turn challenges into opportunities. By the end, you'll understand the forces shaping digital marketing and have actionable strategies to thrive within them. Success in the algorithm game isn't just about visibility; crafting lasting connections and ensuring your brand remains a relevant, trusted voice in the crowded digital space.

Strap in—it's time to learn how to win, adapt, and innovate in an algorithm-driven world.

Understanding LinkedIn's Algorithm Basics

LinkedIn is more than just a professional networking platform; it's a thriving ecosystem where thought leaders, businesses, and professionals share knowledge, ignite conversations, and build relationships. But not every post garners the same attention—some go viral while others barely make it to your connections' feeds. That's where LinkedIn's algorithm steps in, the invisible driver that determines how content is distributed and seen. Understanding its inner workings can completely change how you approach your presence on the platform, transforming how your audience engages with your content.

This book explores LinkedIn's algorithm basics, including how it works, the factors influencing post-performance, and practical strategies for optimizing content for better reach and engagement.

How LinkedIn's Algorithm Works

LinkedIn's algorithm is designed to foster meaningful conversations and professional connections. To this end, it prioritizes content that resonates with users, provides value, and encourages interaction. To achieve this, LinkedIn evaluates and filters content based on specific criteria throughout its distribution pipeline.

The Four-Stage Process

LinkedIn's algorithm operates in stages to determine which posts get the most visibility:

1. **Initial Filtering**

   When you post on LinkedIn, your content undergoes an initial quality check. The algorithm filters out spammy or low-quality content by assessing factors like excessive links, irrelevant hashtags, and repetitive posts.

2. **Engagement Testing**

   After passing the initial filter, your post is shown to a limited audience—usually your first-degree connections. The platform then monitors initial interactions (likes, comments, shares, etc.) to gauge relevance and quality.

3. **Content Scoring**

   The algorithm assigns a score based on how well your post performs in the initial phase. Posts with high engagement rates or positive user signals are prioritized and pushed to a broader audience.

4. **Continual Distribution**

   Finally, LinkedIn continues to evaluate ongoing engagement. Posts that maintain momentum or spark meaningful conversation often see extended visibility beyond the first few hours of posting.

By following this structured approach, LinkedIn ensures that users are exposed to professional, high-value content that aligns with their interests.

Key Factors That Influence LinkedIn's Algorithm

To boost the visibility of your LinkedIn posts, it's essential to understand the key factors the algorithm prioritizes:

1. Content Relevance

The algorithm tailors a user's feed to show content that is aligned with their interests. Factors like your job title, industry, and previous interactions shape the kind of posts you'll see. Creating content relevant to your network's professional preferences increases its chances of being noticed.

2. Engagement Metrics

Engagement—measured by likes, comments, and shares—is one of the strongest indicators of content success. The more people interact with your post, the more likely it is to reach a wider audience.

3. User Interactions and Relationships

LinkedIn prioritizes content from users you've frequently interacted with through comments, messaging, or prior engagement. This is why nurturing genuine relationships on the platform is crucial.

4. Post Type and Format

Specific posts, like native videos, documents, and text-based posts, tend to perform better. LinkedIn also favors "dwell time," meaning how long someone spends reading or interacting with your post. Longer engagement signals value to the algorithm.

5. Hashtags

Hashtags help LinkedIn categorize and distribute your posts to relevant audiences. Using a mix of niche, trending, and branded hashtags can boost visibility if used strategically.

6. Timeliness and Consistency

The time you post and the consistency of your activity affect how often people engage with your content. Regular posting cultivates an active audience ready to interact when you post something new.

Tips to Optimize Content for LinkedIn

1. **Focus on Quality and Value**

    Craft content designed to educate, inspire, or solve a problem for your audience, LinkedIn rewards value-driven posts that encourage conversations.

2. **Leverage Strategic Hashtags**

   Use three to five relevant hashtags per post, combining industry-specific and broader terms. Avoid overloading your content with excessive hashtags, as it can appear spammy.

3. **Encourage Comments and Interactions**

   Ask thought-provoking questions or include a call-to-action (CTA) to spark discussions. The algorithm considers engagement depth, so comments carry more weight than likes.

4. **Post at Optimal Times**

   Analyze your activity to determine when your audience is most active. Typically, weekdays during business hours (e.g., Tuesday or Wednesday morning) work best for professional networks.

5. **Experiment with Content Formats**

   Mix up your posts with videos, infographics, and carousel-style documents, creating higher engagement rates. Keep text posts concise and add formatting like bullet points or line breaks for readability.

6. **Be Consistent but Authentic**

   Post regularly to stay top-of-mind but avoid over-posting or prioritizing quantity over quality. Authenticity fosters trust and deeper connections with your audience.

7. **Participate in Conversations**

   Engagement isn't a one-way street. Actively comment on posts in your feed, acknowledge others in your industry, and show genuine interest in what they share. This engagement increases your visibility within their circles, too.

Benefits of Understanding LinkedIn's Algorithm

Comprehending LinkedIn's algorithm goes far beyond increasing post reach. It is a critical asset in building your personal brand and strengthening professional relationships.

1. Enhanced Visibility

Understanding LinkedIn mechanics enables you to tailor your posts for better reach, helping you stand out in a competitive digital landscape.

2. Deeper Engagement

Consistently generating relevant, engaging content fosters meaningful conversations, leading to lasting relationships with your network.

3. Personal Branding

Whether you're an entrepreneur, job seeker, or thought leader, aligning your content strategy with the algorithm helps reinforce your expertise and credibility.

4. Growth of Professional Network

When your posts resonate with others, they're liked and shared and lead to connections, follower growth, and collaboration opportunities.

5. Business Opportunities

For businesses, reaching a larger audience can translate into leads, partnerships, and customer engagement—vital for organizational success.

Challenges of Staying Ahead

While understanding the algorithm offers advantages, there are challenges, too:

- **Algorithm Changes:** LinkedIn's algorithm evolves frequently, just like any other platform. Staying updated is crucial to remaining effective.
- **Balancing Automation:** While automating some processes may save time, it's essential to avoid overly robotic or generic posts.
- **Maintaining Authenticity:** With strategic optimizations, retaining originality and reflecting your genuine voice to build trust is essential.

In Conclusion

LinkedIn's algorithm is more than just a set of rules dictating post visibility—it's a tool that can elevate your presence on the platform when understood and leveraged correctly. You can keep pace with the algorithm and enjoy greater reach and impact by focusing on content relevance, encouraging meaningful engagement, and staying active within your professional circles.

Success on LinkedIn isn't about hacking the system; it's about creating value-driven content that resonates with your audience while staying true to your unique voice. With a clear strategy and commitment to authenticity, you'll win the algorithm game and forge stronger connections, unlock opportunities, and thrive in the professional networking space.

AI Tools for Optimizing Posting Times and Frequency

Content distribution is a critical part of any successful digital marketing strategy. Knowing the best times to post and how often to share content can significantly impact engagement, reach, and overall campaign success. However, finding the right balance often requires in-depth analysis of audience behavior and platform-specific algorithms—tasks that can be time-consuming and prone to error. This is where artificial intelligence (AI) is revolutionizing how marketers determine optimal posting times and frequencies.

AI-powered tools can analyze complex data sets, provide actionable insights, and automate scheduling, making them indispensable for modern marketers. This book explores how AI tools transform posting strategies, popular tools leading the charge, their benefits, and potential challenges to consider.

How AI Tools Optimize Posting Times and Frequency

AI tools leverage technologies like machine learning, predictive analytics, and data integration to help marketers decide when and how often to post content. Here's how they accomplish this:

1. Audience Behavior Analysis

AI tools can predict audience activity patterns by analyzing historical data. For example, they can identify when your followers are most active on social media, what times email open rates peak, or when website traffic typically spikes. By understanding these patterns, you can schedule posts for times when they'll have the highest visibility.

2. Predictive Analytics

Using machine learning, AI tools can forecast future engagement trends based on past performance. For instance, an AI platform might suggest that posting every Tuesday at 10 a.m. generates 30% more engagement than other days and times. These predictions are continually refined as more data is collected.

3. Platform-Specific Insights

Each digital platform, whether it's Facebook, LinkedIn, Instagram, or WordPress, has different audience dynamics and algorithms. AI tools can analyze platform-specific data to recommend posting schedules tailored to each channel, ensuring maximum impact across all touchpoints.

4. Scheduling Automation

AI tools automate the tedious process of scheduling posts. They don't just queue them but strategically time their publication for optimal performance, eliminating guesswork and manual effort.

5. Real-Time Adjustments

Some advanced AI tools dynamically adjust posting schedules based on real-time data, such as breaking news, a sudden spike in audience activity, or changes in campaign goals.

6. Content Calendars with Intelligent Insights

AI can integrate with content planning tools, enriching calendars with posting frequency and timing recommendations. For example, it might highlight gaps in your strategy or suggest scaling back during periods of low engagement.

Popular AI Tools for Optimizing Posting Strategies

Several cutting-edge AI tools are helping marketers fine-tune their content timing strategies. Here's a look at some of the most popular options and their features:

1. Hootsuite

Hootsuite uses AI-driven analytics to recommend the best times for posting on platforms like Instagram, Facebook, and Twitter. Its "Best Time to Publish" feature analyzes historical performance, industry benchmarks, and audience activity trends.

2. Buffer

Buffer includes an AI-powered scheduling feature called "Optimal Timing Tool." It suggests the best posting times based on audience interaction data. You can also automate and customize your posting frequency across different time zones.

3. Sprout Social

Sprout Social's "ViralPost" technology analyzes audience behavior patterns and engagement data to determine optimal posting times. It continuously updates recommendations, so marketers always have the most current insights.

4. CoSchedule

CoSchedule's AI-based "Best Time Scheduling" feature analyzes past content performance to help you align posts with peak audience activity. It also integrates these recommendations directly into your content calendar.

5. HubSpot

HubSpot offers robust analytics that combines predictive AI and real-time insights. It helps marketers discover when their audiences are most likely to engage and automates posting seamlessly.

6. Tailwind

Tailwind caters primarily to Pinterest and Instagram users. Its "SmartSchedule" feature identifies the ideal posting times for maximizing engagement on visual platforms, making it a favorite for businesses reliant on visual content strategies.

7. Email Campaign Platforms (e.g., Mailchimp, ActiveCampaign)

AI tools in email campaign software analyze subscriber behavior—such as open rates, click-through rates, and time zones—and offer recommendations for optimal email send times.

Benefits of Using AI for Posting Strategies

AI tools provide various benefits for marketers, ranging from improved efficiency to higher engagement rates. Here's how they can give your strategy a competitive edge:

1. Maximized Engagement

AI ensures your content goes live when your audience is most active, making it more likely to be seen, shared, and engaged. This means higher likes, comments, clicks, and conversions.

2. Enhanced Efficiency

AI-driven automation handles the heavy lifting of analyzing, predicting, and scheduling posts. This frees up marketers to focus on creating high-quality content and brainstorming innovative ideas.

3. Data-Driven Confidence

By relying on insights derived from reliable data, AI mitigates the guesswork associated with timing and frequency. Decisions are backed by accurate, actionable analytics.

4. Platform-Specific Optimization

Marketing strategies now span multiple platforms, each with nuanced algorithms and peak activity times. AI customizes posting schedules for each channel, ensuring a tailored approach that resonates with diverse audiences.

5. Improved ROI

Targeted posting minimizes waste. Instead of publishing content that gets lost in low-traffic hours, AI makes each post more effective, driving better results for your investment in time and resources.

6. Predictive Adaptability

AI learns and evolves as more data accumulates. Your posting strategy continually improves, anticipating seasonal changes, engagement patterns, and consumer behavior shifts.

Challenges and Considerations

Despite its clear advantages, using AI to optimize posting times and frequencies isn't without challenges. Here's what marketers should keep in mind:

1. Data Privacy and Security

AI tools often rely on collecting and analyzing user data. It's vital to ensure compliance with data privacy regulations like GDPR and CCPA while maintaining audience trust.

2. The Need for Human Oversight

AI excels at analyzing data, but it lacks human intuition. Marketers should still be involved in final decisions, particularly in maintaining their brand voice and authenticity.

3. Overdependence on Automation

Automating all aspects of content scheduling may lead to robotic, predictable posts. Marketers should balance automation and originality to keep their strategies fresh and engaging.

4. Algorithm Changes

Social media and content platform algorithms evolve frequently. AI tools must keep up with these changes to remain effective, making regular updates and monitoring essential.

Tips for Effectively Using AI Tools

To get the most out of AI tools while avoiding common pitfalls, follow these best practices:

1. **Set Clear Goals**

   Define your goal—more engagement, higher website traffic, or increased email open rates. AI tools are most effective when aligned with specific objectives.

2. **Combine AI with Human Insight**

   While AI handles the technical aspects, human oversight ensures that posts remain authentic, creative, and aligned with your brand's personality.

3. **Regularly Monitor Performance**

   Review analytics to assess whether suggested posting times and frequencies yield the desired results. Adjust strategies and refine settings as necessary.

4. **Experiment and Adjust**

   AI recommendations aren't set in stone. Experiment with different schedules and formats, and use the resulting analytics to improve your strategy further.

5. **Ensure Compliance**

   If your AI tool collects or processes user data, it must comply with all relevant privacy laws and ethical standards.

6. **Maintain Flexibility**

   AI tools can optimize, but real-world events or trending topics sometimes call for unscheduled, spontaneous posts. Be willing to deviate from recommendations when the situation demands.

In Conclusion

AI tools are changing the game for marketers by providing data-driven insights into when and how often to post content. From predictive analytics and audience behavior tracking to scheduling automation, these tools empower marketers to engage their audiences more effectively while saving time and resources.

However, successful implementation requires more than just reliance on technology. Pair AI's precision with your creativity, intuition, and authenticity for a strategy that resonates with your audience while continuously adapting to evolving trends. By mastering the use of AI to optimize posting times and frequency, you'll stay ahead in the fast-paced world of digital marketing, ensuring your content reaches the right people at the right time for maximum impact.

Enhancing Post Engagement Using AI Insights

Engagement is the lifeblood of online content. Whether it's comments on a social media post, likes on a video, or shares of a book, engagement signifies that your audience is consuming your content and connecting with it. However, understanding how to create content that consistently drives engagement can be challenging, especially in an era overloaded with information. This is where artificial intelligence (AI) comes into play, offering powerful tools to analyze audience behavior, identify trends, and refine strategies.

Leveraging AI insights allows businesses, marketers, and creators to target their audiences more effectively, fine-tune their messaging, and significantly boost engagement levels. This book explores how AI can transform your approach to content engagement, the benefits and challenges it presents, and tips for success.

How AI Improves Engagement Analysis

AI tools process vast data to spot patterns, make predictions, and offer actionable recommendations. Here are some key ways in which AI is utilized to analyze and improve engagement:

1. Audience Behavior Analysis

AI tools enable a deep dive into audience behavior. AI identifies what resonates with your audience by analyzing metrics like time spent on posts, interaction types, and follower demographics. For example, it might reveal that your posts perform well on specific days or that certain topics ignite more discussion.

2. Content Performance Tracking

AI evaluates how different pieces of content perform, tracking likes, shares, comments, and click-through rates. With this data, you can determine what content types (e.g., images, videos, or long-form posts) drive better engagement and adjust accordingly.

3. Sentiment Analysis

Sophisticated AI applications can analyze the tone of audience comments and messages, gauging whether your community's feedback is positive, negative, or neutral. This insight helps you refine your voice and tackle potential issues before they escalate.

4. Engagement Trend Predictions

AI identifies emerging trends by monitoring broader audience behaviors and industry dynamics. For example, it can signal a rising demand for video content in your niche or identify current topics generating buzz in your field.

5. Personalized Recommendations

Based on user data, AI tools provide content recommendations tailored to the preferences of individual audience members. For instance, platforms like YouTube and Netflix use AI to suggest videos or shows based on previous user behavior, keeping viewers engaged for longer periods.

6. Real-Time Feedback

AI-powered tools can assess engagement metrics in real time, enabling you to tweak your strategy on the fly. For example, if a live post isn't performing as expected, an AI tool might suggest changing the description or boosting visibility with paid promotion.

Examples of AI Tools for Engagement Insights

Several AI-powered platforms are in charge of helping content creators and marketers enhance engagement. Here's a look at some popular tools and how they work:

1. Sprinklr

Sprinklr provides comprehensive audience insights across multiple digital platforms. Its AI-powered analytics can track audience sentiment, identify trending hashtags, and forecast engagement rates for scheduled posts.

2. Hootsuite's Insights

Hootsuite uses AI to analyze social media trends and recommend optimal posting strategies. Its "Highlights" feature flags top-performing content and identifies patterns in audience interactions.

3. LinkedIn Analytics+

AI backs LinkedIn's advanced analytics function to offer deeper insights into audience demographics, interaction levels, and the professional relevance of posts. It's beneficial for tailoring B2B content strategies.

4. BuzzSumo

BuzzSumo utilizes AI to highlight top-performing content in your niche. It details what's working well for competitors and identifies the type of content driving engagement industry-wide.

5. Google Analytics

Google Analytics employs machine learning to segment audiences and identify which types of content bring visitors back to your site. Its predictive model helps businesses prioritize high-potential engagement opportunities.

6. Canva Magic Write

Integrated into the Canva platform, Magic Write uses AI to provide suggestions for captions, helping marketers craft high-performing social media content that aligns with audience expectations.

Benefits of Using AI for Engagement

AI offers numerous benefits for managing and improving engagement, proving invaluable in today's digital landscape:

1. Precision in Targeting

AI tools help pinpoint your audience's preferences, behaviors, and patterns, enabling you to develop highly tailored content strategies.

2. Enhanced Personalization

Content customized to individual preferences increases engagement. AI enables this level of personalization by gathering insights into user behavior and crafting tailored experiences.

3. Faster Decision-Making

By automating analyzing engagement data, AI provides real-time insights that allow you to make swift decisions about your content strategies.

4. Improved Long-Term Planning

AI helps in the moment and guides longer-term strategies by recognizing patterns and predicting trends that will influence future engagement.

5. Higher ROI

Time saved on manual analysis and the resulting boost in engagement mean better returns on your content creation and promotional efforts.

Challenges of Using AI for Engagement

While AI can be a game-changer, it's essential to understand and mitigate potential challenges:

1. Data Privacy Concerns

Many AI tools rely on user data to provide insights, raising questions about privacy and compliance. It's critical to remain transparent with audiences and adhere to data protection regulations like GDPR and CCPA.

2. Dependence on Algorithms

Over-reliance on AI can lead to content that feels formulaic or lacks creativity. Human oversight is essential to maintaining originality and emotional connection.

3. Keeping Up with Innovation

The pace of AI advancements can make it difficult for marketers to stay current. Regular updates and training are necessary to ensure tools are utilized effectively.

4. Misinterpretation of Insights

AI might offer recommendations that require nuanced interpretation. Marketers should approach insights critically and ensure alignment with their overall brand strategy.

Tips for Effectively Using AI Insights

To truly capitalize on AI's potential for enhancing engagement, keep these best practices in mind:

1. Understand Your Audience

Use AI tools to segment your audience and better understand their needs, preferences, and behavior. The more you know about your audience, the better you can tailor content to resonate with them.

2. Create Data-Driven Content

Base your content strategies on AI-driven insights about what works. For example, if video content historically garners high engagement, consider investing in more multimedia assets.

3. Optimize timing

AI tools often recommend the best times to post based on audience activity. Posting when your audience is most likely engaged ensures your content isn't buried in feeds.

4. Encourage interaction

Structure content with calls-to-action (CTAs) encouraging likes, comments, and shares. AI tools can help refine your CTAs by analyzing what phrasing generates the most interaction.

5. Experiment and Learn

Test different content formats and strategies to determine what resonates best. AI tools work best with ample historical data, so experimentation fuels more accurate recommendations.

6. Balance Automation with Creativity

Allow AI to guide technical strategies like optimizing timing or identifying performance trends while investing your creative energy in storytelling and message development.

7. Stay Ethical

Build trust with your audience by being open about AI use in your strategies and ensuring data privacy and security.

In Conclusion

AI presents unparalleled opportunities for improving engagement in the fast-paced world of digital marketing and content creation. AI tools empower marketers to craft strategies that foster connection and drive results by analyzing audience behavior, providing real-time feedback, and offering precise recommendations.

However, success with AI requires a thoughtful approach. Balancing data-driven insights with human creativity ensures content remains authentic, relatable, and aligned with your brand values. By leveraging AI insights effectively, you can maximize engagement, strengthen relationships with your audience, and stay ahead in the digital age.

Cracking the Algorithm with Real-Time Data Forecasts

Digital algorithms are the invisible hands that shape what we see, click, and engage with online. Whether search engines rank web pages, social media platforms prioritize posts, or video-sharing networks push recommendations, algorithms dictate content visibility. Understanding these algorithms is a critical piece of the puzzle for marketers when crafting strategies to reach audiences effectively. Yet, the fast-paced evolution of these algorithms often creates challenges. Enter real-time data forecasts, a game-changing approach that gives marketers the insights they need to stay ahead of the curve.

This book looks closer at how real-time data forecasts can help marketers adapt to algorithm changes, the tools and techniques that make it happen, the benefits it offers, and the challenges to consider. By mastering this advanced approach, marketers can ensure their content rises above the noise in an increasingly competitive digital landscape.

The Role of Real-Time Data Forecasts in Cracking Algorithms

Algorithms operate on complex decision-making systems that prioritize content that aligns with user interests. However, constant updates and tweaks to these systems make it difficult for marketers to align their strategies. Real-time data forecasts solve this problem by leveraging the power of immediate, relevant, and actionable information to guide decisions.

Here's how real-time data forecasting empowers marketers to understand and adapt to algorithmic changes across platforms like Google, Facebook, and Instagram:

1. Tracking Algorithm Updates as They Happen

When search engines or social media platforms change algorithms, the ripple effect can immediately impact content visibility. Real-time data can flag these changes quickly, allowing marketers to analyze their implications and adjust their strategies before losing engagement or reach.

2. Predicting Trends with Machine Learning

Machine learning models analyze patterns in historical data and apply them to real-time information to predict future trends. For example, a spike in user engagement on a certain type of post or content may hint at an algorithm shift prioritizing that format. Predictive analytics helps marketers proactively align with such trends.

3. Dynamic Content Optimization

Marketers can adjust their content using real-time insights to resonate with current audience preferences or take advantage of fleeting trends. Whether tweaking blog SEO for a search engine change or shifting to short-form video content on social media, real-time forecasts keep strategies agile.

4. Adapting Ad Campaigns on the fly

Real-time data forecasts are particularly valuable for paid ad campaigns. If an algorithm update affects how ads are displayed, forecasts can guide adjustments such as changing target audiences, ad formats, or bidding strategies to minimize wasted ad spend.

Tools and Techniques for Real-Time Data Forecasting

Technology drives the ability to gather and analyze real-time data, providing the foundation for intelligent, accurate forecasts. Below are some tools and techniques marketers can use to harness the power of real-time data forecasting:

1. Google Analytics 4

Google Analytics 4 (GA4) provides real-time insights into website performance, traffic sources, and user behavior. Its predictive metrics, such as purchase probability and churn estimation, allow marketers to anticipate audience actions and better align with search engine updates.

2. Social Listening Platforms

In real-time, tools like Brandwatch and Sprout Social monitor online conversations, trending hashtags, and audience sentiment. These platforms can detect changes in social media algorithms by observing fluctuations in engagement metrics, offering clues for content strategy tweaks.

3. SEO Tools with Real-Time Updates

Platforms like SEMrush and Ahrefs offer real-time keyword tracking and SERP ranking analysis. If an algorithm shift causes a drop in keyword rankings, these tools allow immediate action, such as revising or re-optimizing content.

4. AI-Powered Predictive Analytics Platforms

AI-driven tools like Salesforce Einstein or H2O.ai analyze behavioral data and predict how upcoming changes might influence engagement. This allows marketers to prepare their campaigns for potential algorithm adjustments preemptively.

5. Custom Dashboards and Alerts

Some businesses develop bespoke dashboards to integrate data streams from multiple channels. Alerts can notify marketers of algorithm-related anomalies, such as sudden drops in traffic or engagement, prompting them to investigate and react.

6. Real-Time Ad Bidding Algorithms

Platforms like Google Ads and Facebook Ads Manager for marketers running PPC campaigns offer real-time bidding strategies. These algorithms analyze audience behavior on the spot to adjust bids, ensuring ads reach the right users at the correct times despite alterations in ranking systems.

The Benefits of Using Real-Time Data

Utilizing real-time data forecasts provides numerous advantages that can transform the way marketers approach algorithm management and campaign planning:

1. Improved Visibility

By understanding and adapting to real-time algorithm signals, marketers can position their content where it's most likely to be found. This is especially critical for SEO rankings and social media reach.

2. Higher Engagement

Customizing posts and campaigns based on fresh audience insights leads to more meaningful interactions. Posting at optimal times or sharing trending topics ensures higher engagement rates.

3. Agility in Strategy

Real-time data equips marketers to pivot quickly in response to algorithmic shifts. This keeps their efforts relevant and reduces the risk of spending time and resources on outdated approaches.

4. Optimized Campaign Performance

Forecasts based on real-time data enable better decision-making for paid campaigns, such as choosing the most effective ad placements or formats.

5. Competitive Advantage

While many competitors struggle to keep pace with algorithm changes, leveraging real-time data ensures your strategies remain proactive instead of reactive, giving you a clear edge in the marketplace.

Challenges to Consider

Despite its benefits, using real-time data forecasts also comes with challenges that marketers need to manage effectively:

1. Data Accuracy

Forecasts are only as good as the data they're based on. Relying on incomplete or inaccurate data may lead to flawed insights, underscoring the importance of robust data collection systems.

2. Over-reliance on AI Predictions

AI and machine learning models are powerful but not perfect. Over-relying on automated predictions without human oversight may result in missed opportunities or misaligned strategies.

3. Continuous Monitoring Requirement

Real-time forecasting requires regular monitoring and adjustment, which can be resource-intensive. However, failing to stay engaged can negate the benefits of using these advanced tools.

4. Data Privacy Concerns

Real-time data often involves user behavioral analysis, raising questions about privacy and ethical practices. Marketers must ensure compliance with international data protection standards, such as GDPR and CCPA.

Tips for Effectively Using Real-Time Data Forecasts

Maximizing the benefits of real-time forecasts requires strategic implementation. Here are some best practices to use this technology effectively:

1. Integrate with Existing Tools

Ensure your real-time data platforms are seamlessly integrated with other tools, such as CRM software or campaign management systems, to provide a comprehensive view of engagement metrics.

2. Focus on Key Metrics

Prioritize tracking the metrics most relevant to your goals, such as clicks, conversions, or bounce rates. This avoids data overwhelm and ensures insights are actionable.

3. Combine AI with Human Expertise

Use AI to process data but rely on your team's expertise to interpret findings and weave creative storytelling or unique brand perspectives into campaigns.

4. Stay Agile

Real-time forecasting requires frequent adjustments. Flexibility is key, whether this means shifting content publication times or recalibrating ad strategies.

5. Invest in Training

Ensure your team is well-versed in using forecasting tools. Regular training helps unlock the full potential of these platforms and keeps pace with technological advancements.

6. Monitor Competitors

Real-time tools can also provide insights into competitor activity, helping you learn from their successes and avoid making similar mistakes.

7. Remain Ethical

Always disclose when AI-driven decisions influence advertising or targeting. Employ privacy-first strategies to build trust with your audience.

In Conclusion

Real-time data forecasting is a powerful tool for navigating the complexities of digital algorithms. By combining cutting-edge technology with a strategic approach, marketers can outsmart algorithm changes, drive greater visibility and engagement, and remain competitive in an overcrowded digital space.

While challenges like data accuracy and constant monitoring require attention, the right mix of preparation, flexibility, and ethical practices ensures that real-time data becomes an indispensable asset. By cracking the algorithmic code with real-time insights, marketers can transform their campaigns—from reactive to proactive—and thrive in the evolving digital landscape.

Chapter 7

AI-Powered Analytics for Better Decision-Making

Data is the backbone of modern business. Every interaction, transaction, and activity generates valuable insights that, when harnessed, can inform strategies and shape success. Yet, as the volume and complexity of data multiply, traditional analysis methods are struggling to keep pace. This is where AI-powered analytics is revolutionizing how businesses process information and empowering them to make faster, more intelligent, and more informed decisions.

AI-powered analytics doesn't just crunch numbers; it transforms raw data into meaningful, actionable insights. At its core are technologies like machine learning, predictive analytics, and advanced data visualization, all working to decode patterns, forecast trends, and reveal opportunities that might otherwise remain hidden. Machine learning excels at uncovering intricate patterns across vast datasets, while predictive analytics takes this a step further by forecasting what's likely to come next. Couple that with interactive data visualizations, and businesses are equipped with a new level of clarity—a window into their data that informs and inspires action.

The benefits of integrating AI into analytics are immense. It drives accuracy by reducing the risk of human error, enhances efficiency by automating time-consuming processes, and delivers foresight, allowing businesses to plan proactively rather than reactively. Whether optimizing supply chains, personalizing customer experiences, or carving out competitive advantages, AI analytics touches nearly every facet of business operations.

However, this transformation is not without its challenges. AI demands high-quality data to deliver meaningful insights, raising concerns about data privacy and regulation compliance. Additionally, harnessing the full potential of AI-powered analytics requires skilled personnel who can interpret complex algorithms and integrate them into decision-making frameworks. Businesses must also tackle issues around transparency, ensuring that their AI systems remain explainable and ethical.

This chapter dives deep into the world of AI-powered analytics, unpacking its potential, tools, and implications. We'll explore real-world examples of how industries are leveraging this technology to gain strategic insights while addressing the hurdles they face along the way. By the end, you'll understand why integrating AI analytics isn't just a competitive edge—it's a necessity for thriving in today's data-driven landscape. Prepare to uncover how AI is reshaping the art and science of decision-making, one insight at a time.

Tracking Profile Visits and Post Performance with AI

Social media has evolved from a networking tool to a powerful personal branding, marketing, and business growth platform. To succeed in this dynamic space, it is central to understand how audiences interact with profiles and posts. But tracking these metrics manually can be tedious, time-intensive, and prone to errors. This is where artificial intelligence (AI) steps in, revolutionizing how individuals and businesses monitor profile visits and post-performance to uncover actionable insights and optimize strategies.

This book explores how AI-powered tools can help you monitor and analyze profile visits and posts' performance. From understanding how audiences engage with content to refining strategies for increased reach and relevance, AI has become a game-changer. Below, we discuss the tools, benefits, challenges, and tips for leveraging AI to enhance your social media presence.

How AI Tracks Profile Visits and Post-Performance

AI uses advanced algorithms to collect and analyze massive amounts of data from social media platforms. By pattern recognition and predictive modeling, AI tools can provide in-depth analytics beyond the surface-level metrics offered by traditional analytics dashboards. Here are some ways AI tracks and evaluates profile visits and post-performance:

1. Audience Behavior Insights

AI tools analyze who visits your profile, how often they return, and how they move through your content. For instance, AI might track how long users stay on your page, which posts they engage with the most, and even the flow of clicks leading to your profile. This comprehensive view helps identify your most active audience segments and their preferences.

2. Engagement Metrics

Metrics like likes, comments, shares, and clicks are critical indicators of a post's success. AI tools measure these numbers and analyze patterns, such as the time of day with the highest engagement or which types of posts (e.g., videos, carousels, or stories) perform best with your audience.

3. Content Effectiveness

AI-powered analytics tools can compare the performance of various posts to determine which content themes, tones, and formats deliver the highest engagement. This helps brands refine their strategies to publish more of what resonates and discard what doesn't work.

4. Predictive Analytics

Machine learning enables AI tools to identify trends and predict future success. For instance, an AI system might analyze the trajectory of engagement on a specific post and recommend boosting its visibility with a promotion just before it goes viral.

5. Sentiment Analysis

AI doesn't just measure quantitative metrics; it also evaluates qualitative data by conducting sentiment analysis. By analyzing comments and interactions, AI can gauge whether the feedback is positive, negative, or neutral, providing a more complete picture of audience perceptions.

6. Tracking Link Efficacy

For profiles that use embedded links to drive traffic to websites or landing pages, AI tracks click-through rates (CTR) and conversion metrics, connecting social media activity directly to business outcomes.

Examples of AI Applications for Social Media Analytics

Several AI-powered tools are making headlines for their ability to provide actionable insights into profile visits and post-performance. Here are some popular options:

1. Sprout Social

Sprout Social uses machine learning to analyze engagement data, providing tailored recommendations for when to post and which content themes to focus on. Its reports offer easy-to-read visualizations, which are valuable for making informed strategic decisions.

2. Hootsuite Analytics

Hootsuite's AI capabilities dynamically track engagement metrics over time and recommend ways to optimize performance based on user activity. Additionally, the tool allows for sentiment analysis to understand audience reactions.

3. Socialbakers (Now Part of Emplifi)

Socialbakers harnesses AI to evaluate audience demographics, engagement habits, and content effectiveness. Its predictive features help marketers anticipate content performance trends.

4. Iconosquare

Specializing in Instagram and TikTok, Iconosquare delivers AI-driven insights on audience engagement and profile growth. It highlights which hashtags drive traffic and which time slots result in the highest engagement levels.

5. Google Analytics Social Reports

Although not exclusively AI-driven, Google Analytics incorporates machine learning to connect social media activity (like profile visits or post views) with website interactions, providing a holistic view of traffic flow.

6. ContentStudio

This tool uses AI-driven deep analytics to suggest trending topics, predict post-performance, and refine targeting for more effective posts that align with audience behavior.

Benefits of Using AI for Tracking Profile Visits and Performance

AI tools for social media analytics offer several advantages that make them invaluable for individuals and organizations looking to maximize impact:

1. Improved Targeting

AI's audience behavior insights allow marketers to refine their targeting strategies, ensuring content reaches the most relevant demographics at the right time. This boosts relevance and increases campaign ROI.

2. Content Optimization

Knowing what works and what doesn't enables marketers to double down on successful formats, themes, and tones. AI takes the guesswork out of content creation, narrowing the focus to strategies that yield measurable results.

3. Efficiency and Speed

Real-time data analysis enables quick decision-making. Once a post trends in real-time, AI tools offer suggestions for amplifying its reach— something manual tracking can't achieve as efficiently.

4. Data-Driven Planning

Predictive analytics ensure more strategic planning by forecasting how certain posts or campaigns will likely perform. This advanced foresight leads to better resource allocation and higher engagement rates.

5. Enhanced Decision-Making

AI provides clear, data-backed recommendations. Whether deciding which content to promote, adjusting post frequency, or experimenting with visual styles, AI ensures decisions are grounded in actionable information.

6. Competitive Advantage

While many still work from gut instincts or manual analysis, utilizing AI tools ensures a significant edge over competitors. Access to AI insights accelerates growth and positions users as innovative thought leaders.

Challenges of Using AI for Tracking

Despite its benefits, leveraging AI for tracking profile visits and post-performance comes with challenges:

1. Data Privacy Concerns

AI relies heavily on data collection, raising concerns about how personal information is stored and used. Social media platforms must comply with stringent privacy laws, such as GDPR and CCPA, and users must remain transparent about their methods.

2. Dependence on Algorithms

AI-driven decisions may oversimplify complex human behavior. Blind reliance on algorithms can sometimes lead to generic strategies instead of genuinely creative content.

3. Continuous Updates Needed

AI models require constant updates to remain effective, as social media platforms frequently change their algorithms. Keeping AI tools aligned with platform updates can be an ongoing cost and logistical challenge.

4. Cost and Accessibility

Enterprise-grade AI analytics tools can be expensive, posing barriers for small businesses or individual users. Budget-friendly alternatives may lack advanced predictive capabilities.

5. Interpretation Complexity

AI tools produce detailed reports, sometimes overwhelming users new to analytics or without data science expertise. Skilled personnel are often needed to extract applicable insights.

Tips for Effectively Using AI Tools

To maximize the benefits of AI while mitigating its challenges, follow these tips:

1. Define Clear Goals

Start with specific objectives, such as increasing engagement, boosting profile visits, or refining audience targeting. Clear goals help AI-oriented efforts stay focused and measurable.

2. Combine Creativity with Data

While AI excels at analytics, human creativity is vital for crafting emotionally resonant and authentic content. Strike a balance between data-backed planning and compelling storytelling.

3. Leverage Experimentation

Use AI insights to experiment with different content types, formats, and posting frequencies. Learn from iterations to fine-tune what resonates with your target audience.

4. Track Progress Regularly

Make short-term and long-term tracking a habit. Regular monitoring lets you identify trends early, address weaknesses, and capitalize on emerging opportunities.

5. Prioritize Ethical Practices

Be transparent with audiences about data collection methods and adhere to privacy laws to build trust. Ethical, social media practices ensure longevity and credibility.

6. Invest in Training

Explore online courses or tutorials to understand how to fully interpret AI insights. Many tools offer free resources to familiarize users with their analytics platforms.

In Conclusion

AI has transformed how social media success is measured, allowing users to exceed simple metrics like "likes" and "followers." By employing AI-powered analytics, marketers can gain profound insights into audience behavior, optimize their strategies, and stay ahead in a competitive digital landscape.

However, success requires a thoughtful approach. Combining AI's data-driven precision with human creativity ensures content remains engaging, authentic, and impactful. By integrating AI tools into your social media strategies, you can make smarter decisions, boost engagement, and harness the full potential of your online presence.

Finding High-Value Leads with AI Tools

The quest for high-value leads has always been at the heart of successful sales strategies. However, traditional methods of lead generation can often be time-consuming, imprecise, and inherently limited by human capacity. This is where Artificial Intelligence (AI) emerges, transforming how businesses identify, nurture, and convert valuable leads. By applying machine learning algorithms, predictive analytics, and behavioral insights, AI tools enable sales teams to focus on the most potential leads, maximizing efficiency and driving revenue growth.

This book explores how AI tools are revolutionizing the process of finding high-value leads, their benefits, challenges to be aware of, and best practices for leveraging these tools effectively.

How AI Is Transforming Lead Generation

AI technologies analyze vast quantities of data to uncover patterns and insights that would otherwise be difficult or impossible for humans to discern. Here are some of the ways AI tools are reshaping lead generation:

1. Data-Driven Lead Scoring

Gone are the days of manually scoring leads based on subjective criteria. AI tools now use sophisticated machine learning algorithms to evaluate and rank leads based on their conversion likelihood. By analyzing demographic data, purchasing history, website behavior, and engagement rates, these systems assign scores that help prioritize outreach.

Example: Platforms like HubSpot and Salesforce Einstein use AI-powered lead scoring to help businesses identify which prospects are most likely to become customers.

2. Predictive Analytics

AI tools can analyze historical data to forecast future behaviors and trends. By studying patterns in customer behavior, these tools can predict which leads are most likely to convert and when they're likely to take action. This predictive capability allows sales teams to time their outreach for maximum impact.

Example: Predictive analytics platforms like Leadspace and 6sense provide actionable insights by analyzing intent data, helping businesses tailor their sales strategies.

3. Personalized Outreach

Today's buyers expect personalized interactions, and AI makes this possible on a large scale. AI tools analyze customer data to craft highly customized messages that resonate with each lead's unique needs and preferences. AI ensures every touchpoint feels tailored and relevant, from email campaigns to social media ads.

Example: Tools like Marketo Engage and Drift AI personalize content and automate outreach based on user behavior and preferences, creating a more engaging experience.

4. Behavioral and Predictive Insights

AI tools can track how leads interact with websites, emails, and other content. These behavioral insights allow sales teams to understand a lead's level of interest, identify what content resonates most, and determine the next best step to nurture the relationship.

5. Real-Time Updates and Recommendations

AI tools provide real-time insights into lead activity, allowing businesses to respond quickly. They can notify sales representatives when a lead opens an email, downloads a whitepaper, or visits a pricing page. These timely alerts enable strategic conversations at the right moment to move leads down the sales funnel.

Benefits of Using AI for High-Value Lead Generation

Integrating AI into lead generation offers several key advantages that empower sales teams and improve outcomes:

1. Improved Accuracy and Targeting

AI focuses on data-driven decision-making, eliminating the guesswork in lead generation. It identifies prospects with the highest likelihood of conversion, allowing for more precise targeting and reduced resource wastage.

2. Enhanced Efficiency

By automating time-consuming tasks such as data analysis, lead scoring, and outreach, AI frees sales professionals to spend more time on essential activities like building relationships and closing deals.

3. Better Customer Engagement

With personalized interactions crafted from AI insights, businesses can deliver the right message to the right audience at the right time. This creates a deeper connection with prospects and increases the likelihood of conversion.

4. Higher Conversion Rates

By prioritizing high-value leads and crafting targeted strategies, AI tools ensure that sales teams focus their energy on opportunities that generate revenue.

5. Uncovering Hidden Opportunities

Using traditional methods, AI tools can identify potential customers that might have been overlooked. Through pattern recognition and predictive analytics, they reveal untapped markets and previously unconsidered prospects.

6. Continuous Optimization

AI tools learn and adapt over time, improving the accuracy of lead scoring and recommendations as they process more data. This ensures that lead generation strategies evolve alongside market trends and changing customer behaviors.

Challenges to Consider

Despite their many advantages, AI tools for lead generation come with their own set of challenges that businesses need to address:

1. Data Privacy Concerns

AI tools rely heavily on customer data to make accurate predictions and recommendations. This raises questions about data privacy and compliance with regulations such as GDPR and CCPA. Businesses must ensure that they handle sensitive information responsibly and transparently.

2. Complexity and Expertise

Successfully implementing and managing AI tools requires technical expertise. Sales teams must be trained to use these tools effectively, and businesses may need to hire specialists to oversee their AI systems. While AI simplifies some processes, its technical requirements can pose a barrier to entry for smaller organizations.

3. Bias in Algorithms

AI tools are only as good as the data they're trained on. If the input data contains biases, the output recommendations may reflect those biases, potentially leading to missteps or missed opportunities. Businesses must actively monitor and mitigate biases to ensure that AI tools deliver fair and accurate results.

4. Over-Reliance on Technology

AI tools are powerful but not infallible. Over-relying on them without human oversight can lead to losing personal connections in sales and missed opportunities to build meaningful relationships.

Tips for Effectively Using AI Tools to Find High-Value Leads

To maximize the benefits of AI in lead generation, businesses should consider the following best practices:

1. Start with Clean and Comprehensive Data

AI tools require accurate and up-to-date data to deliver reliable insights. Regularly audit your customer database to ensure it's free of errors and complete.

2. Align AI Insights with Sales Strategies

Rather than replacing human intuition, use AI insights to inform and enhance your sales strategies. For the best results, combine AI recommendations with the expertise and experience of your sales team.

3. Set Clear Goals

Define specific objectives for your AI-powered lead generation efforts. Whether aiming to improve engagement rates, shorten the sales cycle, or boost revenue, having clear goals will help guide your AI implementation.

4. Invest in Training and Support

Equip your sales team with the skills they need to leverage AI tools effectively. Provide ongoing training and access to support resources to ensure they feel confident using these technologies.

5. Regularly Evaluate and Adjust

AI tools need continuous monitoring and optimization to stay effective. Analyze performance metrics regularly to identify areas for improvement and adjust your strategies as needed.

6. Maintain Ethical Standards

Always prioritize ethical practices when using AI for lead generation. Ensure that your use of data complies with legal regulations and respects customer privacy.

In Conclusion

AI tools have fundamentally changed how businesses approach lead generation, making the process more efficient, targeted, and data-driven. By precisely identifying high-value leads and delivering personalized outreach strategies, AI enables sales teams to focus their energy where it matters most. However, to fully capitalize on the potential of these tools, businesses must approach their implementation thoughtfully, addressing challenges like data privacy, algorithmic bias, and the need for expertise.

By integrating AI insights into your sales processes, regularly refining your strategies, and balancing automation with human interaction, you can transform your lead generation efforts into a growth powerhouse. With the right approach, AI has the potential not only to find but convert high-value leads, driving success in today's competitive marketplace.

Personalizing Sales Pitches Using AI Insights

Sales success hinges on connection—understanding your audience and delivering a message that resonates with their needs, goals, and preferences. However, in a competitive market, generic sales strategies often fail to capture attention or build trust. Enter Artificial Intelligence (AI), a powerful tool that's transforming how sales teams tailor their pitches. By providing deep insights into customer preferences and behaviors, AI empowers businesses to create highly personalized sales interactions that engage and compel action.

This book explores how AI is revolutionizing the art of personalization in sales pitches. From explaining the technologies behind these innovations to detailing the benefits and challenges, we'll guide you through the practical ways to incorporate AI insights into your sales strategies.

The Role of AI in Personalizing Sales Pitches

AI technologies excel at analyzing vast amounts of data to uncover meaningful patterns and actionable insights. When it comes to personalizing sales pitches, AI systems tap into a wide range of data sources—such as customer purchase histories, browsing behaviors, social media activity, and previous interactions—to create a rich profile of each client or prospect.

Here's how AI is specifically transforming sales pitches:

1. Behavioral Analysis

AI tools track and analyze customer behavior across multiple channels. For example, if a prospect frequently interacts with a specific product page, it signals a potential area of interest. By understanding these behaviors, sales teams can tailor pitches to highlight features or benefits that directly address the prospect's needs.

2. Segmentation and Profiling

Traditional segmentation strategies group prospects based on limited metrics like demographics or geography. Conversely, AI dives deeper—profiling customers based on factors such as interests, buying patterns, and even sentiment analysis gleaned from interactions. This enables ultra-targeted approaches that are far more effective.

3. Dynamic Personalization

AI tools allow for dynamic personalization by continuously updating customer profiles in real-time. For example, if a prospect engages with specific content or shows new purchase behavior, AI adjusts its insights so sales teams can align their pitches accordingly.

4. Predictive Insights

AI-powered predictive analytics tools assess past data to forecast future customer preferences. For instance, based on purchasing trends, AI can predict when a customer might need to reorder a product or upgrade to a new service, ensuring timely and relevant outreach.

5. Content Customization

AI platforms like Drift or Outreach can generate personalized content recommendations from email pitches to face-to-face presentations. These platforms ensure that every communication element—content, tone, timing—aligns with the recipient's preferences.

AI Tools and Platforms for Personalizing Sales Pitches

Many AI-powered sales tools are available to help businesses unlock the potential for personalization. Some popular platforms include:

- **Salesforce Einstein:** Offers AI-driven insights for better customer understanding and tailored interactions within the CRM system.
- **HubSpot:** Provides predictive lead scoring and content suggestions based on customer data and engagement behaviors.
- **Gong.io:** Analyzes conversations to identify key questions, objections, and buying signals, allowing reps to tailor their follow-up strategies.
- **Conversica:** Leverages AI to engage leads with two-way, human-like emails designed to nurture prospects based on their interests.
- **Crayon:** Tracks real-time market and competitive intelligence to provide contextually personalized messaging for prospects.

These tools remove much guesswork from sales pitches, allowing sales representatives to approach prospects confidently and precisely.

Benefits of Personalizing Sales Pitches with AI Insights

AI-driven personalization doesn't just save time—it creates tangible business value across key areas of the sales process. Here are some of the standout benefits:

1. Enhanced Customer Engagement

Personalized pitches capture attention by directly addressing the customer's pain points and goals. AI insights make every interaction relevant, fostering a stronger connection between the salesperson and the prospect.

2. Improved Conversion Rates

When leads feel understood, they're more likely to take action. AI-enabled personalization significantly increases the effectiveness of sales pitches, improving conversion rates and reducing the time it takes to close deals.

3. Stronger Customer Relationships

AI allows for more informed conversations by providing reps with rich, context-specific insights. This enhances relationship-building, turning first-time buyers into loyal, long-term customers.

4. Efficient Resource Allocation

AI prioritizes high-value leads most likely to convert, allowing sales teams to focus their energy on opportunities that deliver the greatest ROI.

5. Real-Time Adaptability

AI tools keep customer profiles and recommendations updated in real-time. This dynamic flexibility ensures that sales pitches remain relevant despite changing customer circumstances.

6. Uncovering New Opportunities

By analyzing historical and behavioral data, AI tools can reveal untapped needs or preferences that sales teams might not have identified otherwise.

Overcoming Challenges

While the benefits of AI in personalizing sales pitches are clear, businesses must address specific challenges to make the most of this technology:

1. Data Privacy Concerns

Personalization requires collecting and analyzing sensitive customer data, raising concerns about privacy and compliance. To mitigate these risks, businesses must adopt transparent data policies and invest in robust security measures.

2. Complexity of Implementation

Integrating AI tools into existing workflows can be complex, requiring alignment between IT, sales, and marketing teams. Proper training is essential for maximizing tool usage.

3. Dependence on Data Quality

AI systems are only as good as the data they analyze. Poor-quality data can lead to incorrect insights and ineffective personalization efforts.

4. Bias in Algorithms

AI algorithms can unintentionally reinforce biases present in training data. Businesses must regularly audit and refine their AI systems to ensure fair and accurate results.

5. Cost of Adoption

The upfront investment in AI tools may seem daunting for smaller organizations. However, businesses need to weigh these costs against AI's long-term value in improved sales outcomes.

Tips for Effectively Using AI Insights in Sales Pitches

To fully leverage AI's potential for personalization, businesses should consider the following best practices:

1. Integrate AI with Your CRM System

Link your AI tools to your CRM to centralize customer data and ensure insights are accessible to the sales team. This integration enhances collaboration and consistency in sales strategies.

2. Regularly Update Data

Keep customer profiles and datasets up to date. Continuous updating ensures AI insights remain accurate and relevant, enabling more effective personalization.

3. Combine AI with Human Intuition

While AI provides actionable insights, sales reps must use their judgment to frame and deliver pitches with authenticity and empathy.

4. Focus on Customer-Centric Strategies

Make the customer the hero of your sales pitch. Use AI insights to showcase your product's features and demonstrate how it aligns with the customer's goals.

5. Monitor performance

Track the effectiveness of AI-powered sales pitches. Use analytics to identify what's working and tweak strategies based on performance metrics.

6. Invest in Training

Ensure that sales reps are trained to use AI tools effectively. Understanding how to interpret AI-generated insights is as important as having access to the technology.

7. Adhere to Ethical Standards

Implement AI personalization responsibly. Ensure all customer data is handled securely and used in ways that reflect your brand's commitment to ethical standards.

In Conclusion

Personalizing sales pitches using AI insights is no longer a luxury—it's quickly becoming necessary in the modern business landscape. Businesses can foster deeper connections, improve conversion rates, and create lasting customer relationships by leveraging AI tools to analyze customer data, craft tailored messages, and predict future needs.

However, achieving success with AI-powered personalization requires thoughtful implementation, a willingness to adapt, and a commitment to balancing technology with a human touch. When done right, using AI insights for sales personalization isn't just a strategy—it's a game-changer for growth.

Tracking and Nurturing Leads with AI CRM Systems

Tracking and nurturing leads has always been a fundamental aspect of successful sales and marketing. However, with the surge in digital transformation and the sheer volume of customer data available today, traditional methods often fall short. Enter Artificial Intelligence (AI)-powered Customer Relationship Management (CRM) systems—game-changing tools that are revolutionizing how businesses manage their leads. From automating routine tasks to delivering predictive insights and enabling personalized communication, AI CRM systems are reshaping lead management profoundly.

This book explores how AI-driven CRM systems streamline and enhance lead tracking and nurturing processes. We'll examine their benefits, challenges, and best practices to help businesses maximize this powerful technology.

The Role of AI in Lead Tracking and Nurturing

AI-powered CRM systems use advanced algorithms and machine learning to process vast amounts of data, uncovering actionable insights and automating repetitive tasks. When applied to lead tracking and nurturing, these systems go beyond simple contact management, transforming how businesses identify, engage, and follow up with potential customers.

Here's how AI enhances lead management:

1. Automated Lead Tracking

AI CRM systems automatically collect and organize data from various sources, such as website activity, email interactions, social media engagements, and customer service queries. By centralizing and streamlining lead tracking, these systems eliminate manual processes and provide teams with a holistic view of each prospect's activity.

Example: Tools like Salesforce Einstein and Zoho CRM gather and analyze lead data in real-time, ensuring sales teams have up-to-date information to inform their strategies.

2. Predictive Lead Scoring

Not all leads are created equal, and prioritizing the right ones is crucial. AI CRM systems use predictive analytics to score leads based on their conversion likelihood. By analyzing historical data, behavior patterns, and demographic information, AI identifies high-value prospects, allowing sales teams to focus their efforts where it matters most.

Example: HubSpot's AI-enhanced CRM assigns lead scores based on engagement metrics, giving sales reps a clear roadmap for prioritization.

3. Personalized Follow-Up and Nurturing

AI CRM systems facilitate personalized communication by analyzing customer preferences, behaviors, and needs. Whether crafting tailored email content or suggesting optimal timing for outreach, AI ensures that every interaction feels relevant and meaningful.

Example: ActiveCampaign uses AI to automate personalized email sequences, nurturing prospects through customized touchpoints that align with their interests.

4. Real-Time Insights and Notifications

With AI-enabled real-time tracking, teams can monitor lead activity as it happens. Notifications alert sales reps when a lead takes a significant action, such as visiting a pricing page or downloading a whitepaper. These timely updates enable immediate, targeted follow-ups that keep prospects engaged.

Example: Pipedrive integrates AI capabilities to provide real-time insights and reminders, ensuring no lead gets overlooked during critical moments in the sales process.

5. Streamlined Task Management

AI CRM systems relieve sales teams of the burden of managing repetitive tasks by automating actions like scheduling follow-ups, sending reminders, and updating lead statuses. This allows teams to focus on building relationships and closing deals.

Benefits of Using AI CRM Systems

Integrating AI into CRM systems offers transformative benefits for lead tracking and nurturing:

1. Improved Lead Tracking Efficiency

By automating data collection and organization, AI CRM systems reduce the time and effort required to monitor leads. Sales teams spend less time on administrative tasks and more time on value-added activities.

2. Enhanced Lead Quality

Predictive lead scoring ensures that sales efforts are directed toward prospects with the highest potential, improving conversion rates and optimizing resource allocation.

3. Personalized Customer Experiences

AI enables businesses to deliver highly tailored communication throughout the customer journey. Personalized outreach builds trust, strengthens relationships, and increases the likelihood of conversion.

4. Actionable Insights

AI analyzes customer behavior and market trends to provide actionable insights. These insights help businesses refine their strategies and anticipate customer needs.

5. Faster Response Times

Real-time notifications and automated workflows ensure that businesses respond promptly to lead activity, keeping prospects engaged and minimizing the risk of losing opportunities to competitors.

6. Cost and Time Savings

Automation not only increases efficiency but also reduces operational costs. AI CRM systems free up valuable time and resources by handling repetitive tasks and streamlining processes.

Challenges to Address

Despite their many advantages, using AI CRM systems comes with challenges that businesses must carefully manage:

1. Data Privacy Concerns

AI CRM systems rely heavily on customer data to provide meaningful insights. Businesses must ensure compliance with data protection regulations (e.g., GDPR, CCPA) and build customer trust by implementing robust privacy policies.

2. Need for Skilled Personnel

Implementing and managing AI CRM systems requires technical expertise. Businesses may need to invest in training or hire specialists to oversee these tools.

3. Integration Complexity

Integrating AI CRM systems with existing sales and marketing workflows can be challenging. Proper planning and execution are essential to avoid disruptions.

4. Dependence on Data Quality

AI's effectiveness depends on the quality of the data it processes. Businesses must prioritize data accuracy, completeness, and relevance to ensure reliable insights.

5. Cost of Adoption

While AI-powered CRM systems offer long-term value, the initial investment can be significant. Businesses, especially smaller ones, may face budget constraints when adopting these tools.

Tips for Effectively Using AI CRM Systems

To fully leverage AI CRM systems for lead tracking and nurturing, businesses should consider these best practices:

1. Start with Clean Data

Ensure that your CRM system is populated with accurate, up-to-date data. Conduct regular audits to maintain data integrity and eliminate duplicates or errors.

2. Integrate AI Into Your Workflow

Align AI CRM insights with existing sales and marketing processes. Ensure that your team can access relevant data and understand how to incorporate AI recommendations into their strategies.

3. Invest in Training

Provide your team with training on how to use AI-powered CRM tools effectively. Build their confidence in interpreting AI-generated insights and leveraging them for decision-making.

4. Set Clear Goals

Define specific objectives for your AI CRM initiatives. Whether improving lead conversion rates, reducing response times, or enhancing customer satisfaction, having clear goals ensures focused implementation.

5. Use Automation Wisely

Automate repetitive tasks but maintain a human touch in customer interactions. Strike a balance between efficiency and personalization to foster genuine relationships.

6. Monitor and Refine

Regularly review the performance of your AI-driven CRM system. Use analytics to identify areas for improvement and refine your strategies based on real-world results.

7. Prioritize Ethical Practices

Be transparent about how you collect and use customer data. Prioritize ethical practices to build trust and maintain compliance with legal regulations.

In Conclusion

AI CRM systems represent a significant leap forward in tracking and nurturing leads. These tools give businesses a distinct competitive edge by automating processes, delivering actionable insights, and enabling personalized communication. While challenges like data privacy and implementation complexity require careful consideration, the benefits outweigh the hurdles.

When implemented thoughtfully, AI CRM systems can transform lead management from a manual, time-intensive task into a streamlined, intelligence-driven process that fuels growth. For businesses looking to stay ahead of the curve, now is the time to harness the power of AI to track, nurture, and convert high-value leads with greater efficiency and precision.

Enhancing Outreach Efficiency and Conversion Rates

Effective outreach is the bedrock of successful sales and marketing. It's about connecting with the right audience at the right time and using the right message to drive conversions. However, with increasing competition and an abundance of data, traditional outreach methods are often too slow or inefficient to yield the desired results. Leveraging modern strategies and technologies can dramatically transform outreach efforts, making them faster, more innovative, and more impactful.

This book discusses enhancing outreach efficiency and conversion rates through automation, personalization, data analysis, and strategic implementation. We explore the tools, benefits, challenges, and best practices to help businesses optimize their communication efforts.

Modern Strategies for Outreach Efficiency

Technology has changed the game for outreach. Rather than relying on manual processes, today's businesses can automate and optimize workflows to touch more prospects more precisely. Here are some key strategies that can elevate outreach efforts:

1. Automating Outreach Processes

Automation tools allow businesses to streamline their outreach campaigns. Whether sending personalized emails, scheduling follow-ups, or posting on social media, automation removes repetitive tasks while keeping interactions timely.

Example: Platforms like Mailchimp and ActiveCampaign can schedule and personalize email campaigns at scale. Tools like Hootsuite automate social media posts for consistent outreach across multiple channels.

2. Personalizing Communication

Customers are more likely to engage with outreach efforts when messages feel tailor-made for them. Personalization involves leveraging data—browsing history, past purchases, or demographic details—to craft communications that address individual preferences and needs.

Example: AI tools like Segment and Marketo Engage analyze customer behavior to create personalized email and content recommendations.

3. Utilizing AI and Predictive Analytics

AI technologies excel at analyzing large datasets to uncover patterns and trends. By understanding customer behavior, AI-powered tools generate predictive insights that guide outreach efforts' targeting and timing.

Example: AI platforms like HubSpot and Salesforce Einstein deploy predictive analytics to identify leads with the highest likelihood of conversion, ensuring outreach resources are allocated efficiently.

4. Multi-Channel Outreach

Reaching customers across multiple channels—such as email, social media, SMS, and direct mail—can dramatically improve engagement rates. Multi-channel campaigns ensure that your brand stays top-of-mind and captures attention on your audience's platforms.

Example: Tools like Intercom and Klaviyo enable businesses to run synchronized campaigns across diverse channels.

5. A/B Testing and Optimization

Continuous testing is essential for refining outreach campaigns. A/B testing allows businesses to experiment with different messages, subject lines, visuals, and CTAs to determine what resonates most with their audience.

Example: Platforms like Optimizely and Google Optimize support A/B testing, helping businesses refine their outreach strategies based on real-time performance data.

Benefits of Enhanced Outreach Efficiency

Adopting cutting-edge tools and strategies for outreach saves time and creates a ripple effect of positive outcomes for sales and marketing teams.

1. Time Savings

Automation reduces the burden of repetitive tasks like email scheduling and data entry, freeing up time for more strategic work. Sales and marketing teams can focus on activities that require creativity and human interaction.

2. Improved Targeting

Personalized outreach ensures that businesses connect with prospects most likely to convert. With AI and data analytics, teams can prioritize high-value leads and deliver relevant messaging to the right audience segments.

3. Higher Conversion Rates

When done effectively, tailored communication and multi-channel campaigns lead to stronger prospect engagement and higher conversion rates. Customers are more willing to respond when they sense a genuine interest in their needs.

4. Better Customer Engagement

Continuous, meaningful interactions build trust and create deeper connections with customers. AI-driven personalization and timely follow-ups make prospects feel valued, increasing their likelihood of becoming loyal buyers.

5. Scalability

With automation, businesses can scale their outreach efforts without requiring proportional resource increases. This is particularly advantageous for small teams looking to make a big impact.

6. Data-Driven Decisions

The ability to track performance metrics—such as open rates, click-through rates, and response times—allows businesses to refine their strategies based on measurable outcomes, ensuring continuous improvement.

Challenges to Be Aware Of

While enhancing outreach efficiency delivers significant benefits, there are challenges that businesses must address to make the most of these opportunities:

1. Data Privacy Concerns

With the increased reliance on customer data to personalize messages, businesses must comply with data protection regulations like GDPR and CCPA. Transparent data usage policies are essential to building customer trust.

2. Technical Expertise

Adopting tools like AI platforms or advanced CRMs often requires technical knowledge that teams may lack. Investing in training or hiring skilled personnel is key to maximizing the effectiveness of these tools.

3. Implementation Complexity

Integrating new tools into existing workflows can be complex, especially when syncing data across different systems. A poorly executed integration can disrupt operations and limit the potential of outreach campaigns.

4. Cost of Adoption

While the long-term ROI of automation and AI tools is often worth it, the upfront investment may be a barrier for some businesses, particularly smaller ones.

5. Over-Automation Risks

While automation improves efficiency, there is a risk of losing the human touch. Over-relying on automated messaging can result in impersonal communications that fail to resonate with customers.

Tips for Effective Outreach and Conversion

To make the most of outreach activities and boost conversion rates, follow these best practices:

1. Integrate AI with Your CRM

Align your AI tools with your CRM system to centralize customer data and gain better insights into lead behavior. This ensures a cohesive approach to outreach and follow-up.

2. Continuously Update Customer Profiles

Keep customer data accurate and current. Regularly update profiles with new interactions, purchases, and preferences to ensure outreach remains relevant.

3. Focus on Quality Over Quantity

Avoid sending generic messages to a wide audience. Instead, prioritize high-value leads and craft personalized communications to maximize your chances of success.

4. Test and Refine Regularly

Leverage A/B testing to optimize your campaigns' content, timing, and channels. Use feedback loops to refine outreach strategies based on what works best.

5. Maintain a Human Touch

While automation is functional, adding a personal element to your communications is essential. Human interaction builds trust and fosters stronger relationships.

6. Train Your Team on New Tools

Invest in training programs to upskill your sales and marketing teams to effectively use technologies like AI tools, CRMs, and data analytics dashboards.

7. Ensure compliance

Stay ahead of data privacy regulations by implementing secure systems and adhering to ethical practices in data usage.

8. Measure Performance Metrics

Track key KPIs such as response rates, lead conversion rates, and ROI from outreach campaigns. Use these insights to fine-tune your strategy over time.

In Conclusion

Enhancing outreach efficiency and boosting conversion rates are non-negotiable goals for businesses looking to thrive in today's competitive marketplace. Companies can optimize their outreach efforts by leveraging automation, personalization, and AI-driven insights and create meaningful connections with prospects.

However, success requires more than just adopting new technologies—thoughtful implementation, continuous refinement, and a customer-centric approach. Businesses can transform their outreach efforts and drive sustained growth with the right balance of strategy, tools, and human touch.

Bonus
Download

SCAN ME

Chapter 8
Staying Ahead of AI Trends

Artificial Intelligence (AI) is more than a technological revolution; it's a defining force reshaping industries, economies, and societies. AI innovation is relentless, with groundbreaking developments emerging almost daily. Businesses that fail to keep up risk falling behind in a fast-moving marketplace. Staying ahead of AI trends isn't just about leveraging technology—it's a strategic imperative for maintaining relevance and competitive advantage in an increasingly AI-driven world.

This chapter explores why staying informed about AI advancements is critical for business success. AI's influence spans from automating routine operations to revolutionizing customer interactions, enabling data-driven decisions, and unlocking new possibilities for innovation. By understanding and adopting the latest trends, businesses can refine their strategies, improve operational efficiency, and explore untapped opportunities.

However, keeping up with AI advancements isn't without its challenges. The sheer speed of technological change can feel overwhelming, and organizations must commit to continuous learning to stay current. Developing the expertise required to evaluate, implement, and manage AI tools is no small task. Yet, those willing to invest the effort will be better positioned to adapt to future disruptions, seize emerging opportunities, and lead their industries forward.

This chapter highlights the benefits of staying ahead of AI trends and provides practical insights on how to proactively monitor, learn, and apply the latest AI technologies. It emphasizes the importance of cultivating a forward-thinking mindset and fostering a culture of innovation within your organization. Whether you're leading a startup or steering a multinational company, understanding the trajectory of AI is essential for navigating the complexities of tomorrow's business landscape.

We'll explore the tools and strategies that can help you anticipate where AI is heading, how to evaluate which trends align with your business goals, and ways to implement those advancements effectively. Ultimately, staying ahead of AI trends isn't just about adopting the latest tools—it's about envisioning and creating a future where your business can thrive in an AI-powered world.

Current AI Tools That Are Transforming LinkedIn

LinkedIn has become the go-to professional platform for networking, job hunting, and personal branding. But if you've been paying attention, you've likely noticed how artificial intelligence (AI) has revolutionized the LinkedIn experience. From smarter job recommendations to automated networking features, AI tools are making it easier than ever for users to unlock the full potential of this platform.

This book dives into how AI is transforming the way professionals use LinkedIn. We'll explore key AI-driven tools and features already reshaping the platform, the benefits these innovations bring, and the challenges they pose. Additionally, we'll provide actionable tips to help you use AI to maximize your LinkedIn opportunities.

How AI is Shaping the LinkedIn Experience

With its rich database of professionals, industries, and thought leaders, LinkedIn is an ideal environment for AI to thrive. The platform has integrated AI into its core features, while third-party tools further enhance the experience. Here's how AI is transforming LinkedIn:

1. Personalized Content Recommendations

Gone are the days of aimlessly scrolling through your feed, hoping to find relevant content. LinkedIn's AI algorithms analyze user behavior—such as the posts you engage with, the books you read, and the hashtags you follow—to curate a feed tailored to your interests. This ensures you stay updated on industry trends, thought leadership, and opportunities that matter to you.

Example: LinkedIn's "Discover More" feature suggests topics, creators, and content based on your professional interests, helping you stay informed without the effort of manual searching.

2. Smarter Job Matching

LinkedIn's AI-powered job recommendations simplify the search process for job seekers. By analyzing your profile, skills, and activity, LinkedIn's algorithms suggest roles that align with your experience and career goals. AI also provides insights into how well your profile matches a particular job posting and suggests areas for improvement.

Example: Features like "Jobs You May Be Interested In" and tailored alerts for job openings increase the chances of finding roles suited to your expertise.

3. Automated Messaging and Outreach

Networking on LinkedIn just got smarter with AI. AI-driven tools now help users personalize connection requests and introductory messages. Instead of generic "Hi, I'd like to connect" messages, AI tools craft contextually relevant outreach based on the recipient's profile and shared connections.

Example: Tools like Crystal use AI to analyze someone's LinkedIn profile and craft messages that match their professional tone, increasing the likelihood of positive responses.

4. AI Profile Optimization

Your LinkedIn profile is often the first impression you make professionally. AI-powered tools now provide insights into optimizing your profile for better visibility, relevance, and attractiveness to recruiters. From suggesting keyword enhancements to identifying gaps in your experience, these tools ensure your profile stands out.

Example: LinkedIn's built-in AI prompts for profile improvement—like adding a professional headline or skills—help increase your "searchability" to recruiters and industry peers.

5. AI Writing Assistance

Creating engaging posts or books on LinkedIn can be challenging, particularly for those who don't consider themselves writers. AI writing assistants help craft impactful updates, professional "About" summaries and even thought leadership books.

Example: Tools like Jasper or Grammarly work alongside LinkedIn by using AI to refine your communication and ensure your content resonates with your audience.

6. Sentiment Analysis for Engagement

AI is helping marketers and professionals better understand audience reactions. Sentiment analysis tools evaluate how people respond to your posts, offering insights on what works and what doesn't. This data can guide future communication strategies for better engagement.

Example: Analytics extensions like Shield integrate AI to break down audience sentiment, providing actionable insights into how to optimize your LinkedIn content.

7. Talent Insights for Recruiters

For recruiters, LinkedIn's AI tools like Talent Insights analyze hiring needs, job market trends, and candidate databases. This enables highly effective recruitment campaigns that find suitable candidates and maximize employer branding.

Example: Talent Insights generates data visualizations showing hiring trends and talent supply, which recruiters can use to refine their talent acquisition strategies.

Benefits of AI Tools on LinkedIn

AI is helping LinkedIn users—from job seekers to recruiters—accomplish more quickly. Here are some of the most impactful benefits of AI tools on LinkedIn:

1. Time Efficiency

AI-powered automation accelerates job searching, profile optimization, and outreach, allowing users to focus on building relationships and following leads.

2. Better Engagement

With AI tools curating personalized feeds and crafting tailored messages, users experience higher engagement with their network, posts, and job applications.

3. Enhanced Visibility

AI's recommendations to optimize your profile ensure you appear in more searches, whether by recruiters, potential clients, or collaborators.

4. Improved Networking

AI insights remove much guesswork from initiating connections by analyzing contexts and suggesting meaningful ways to engage.

5. Data-Driven Decision Making

By leveraging analytics, users can refine their approach to content creation, networking, and branding based on what resonates with their audience.

6. Better Job Matching

AI considerably narrows the gap between skills and opportunities for job seekers, producing matches that cater specifically to individual goals.

Challenges of Using AI Tools on LinkedIn

Despite the powerful benefits, leveraging AI on LinkedIn isn't without challenges. Here are some of the key barriers users may face:

1. Data Privacy Concerns

LinkedIn's AI tools rely heavily on personal data, sparking concerns about how this information is collected, stored, and used. Users must balance the use of AI-powered services with an understanding of data privacy regulations.

2. Reduced Human Touch

AI-driven automated communication risks losing the personalized human interaction on which LinkedIn was founded. Overusing automation can make your communication feel impersonal or robotic.

3. Learning Curve

Adopting LinkedIn's AI tools effectively may require a degree of technical literacy. Users unfamiliar with AI could struggle to implement and benefit from these technologies.

4. Algorithm Bias

AI systems, while powerful, are subject to algorithmic biases that may inadvertently limit exposure to diverse opportunities or profiles.

Tips for Effectively Using AI Tools on LinkedIn

To make the most of AI tools and features on LinkedIn, follow these best practices:

1. Leverage AI Insights for Content Creation

Use AI-generated recommendations to fine-tune your content. Ensure posts and books provide value to your audience while aligning with industry trends.

2. Optimize Your Profile Regularly

Continuously refine your LinkedIn profile based on AI suggestions. Keeping your profile dynamic and relevant increases its visibility to recruiters and collaborators.

3. Strike a Balance with Automation

Use AI to amplify your efforts—but don't go overboard. Maintain a balance between automating efforts and infusing genuine human interactions into your networking.

4. Understand Analytics

Dive into analytics insights provided by AI to grasp what drives engagement. Use these data points to influence your posting schedule, content style, and outreach methods.

5. Be Mindful of Privacy

Before adopting third-party AI tools, thoroughly review their privacy policies to ensure your data is being handled responsibly. Know what you're agreeing to when authorizing access to your LinkedIn account.

6. Build a Personalized Strategy

Instead of following generic advice, tailor your use of AI tools to align with specific goals, such as landing a job, increasing visibility, or scaling your network.

In Conclusion

Artificial intelligence is changing how we approach professional networking and branding on LinkedIn. By streamlining tasks like job searching, content curation, and personalized outreach, AI tools provide unparalleled opportunities for LinkedIn users to succeed. However, as with any technology, its effectiveness depends on thoughtful implementation and mindful usage.

Adapt to these AI innovations and continually refine your strategy to stay competitive. When used effectively, LinkedIn's AI tools can become your most powerful ally in achieving your professional goals—whether you're building a personal brand, expanding your network, or landing your dream job.

Emerging AI Technologies and What They Mean for LinkedIn Users

Artificial Intelligence (AI) continues to redefine industries, and LinkedIn is no exception. Emerging AI technologies are transforming how users interact with the platform, making networking, job searching, and content sharing smarter and easier than ever. From advanced algorithms that craft highly relevant job recommendations to AI tools that help professionals build their personal brands, LinkedIn is rapidly evolving into an AI-powered ecosystem.

This book explores the cutting-edge AI technologies shaping LinkedIn, the benefits they bring, and the challenges they pose. Whether you're a job seeker, recruiter, marketer, or thought leader, understanding these advancements is essential for staying ahead and making the most of LinkedIn.

Emerging AI Technologies at Play

Numerous AI innovations are changing the game for LinkedIn users. Here's a closer look at how specific technologies are making their mark:

1. Natural Language Processing (NLP)

NLP enables LinkedIn to understand and generate human-like text. This technology enhances content recommendations by interpreting users' preferences, analyzing conversations, and tailoring recommendations for posts, groups, and connections.

Example: LinkedIn uses NLP to suggest keywords and phrases when crafting summaries, headlines, or messages. AI tools also analyze a user's messages to provide suggestions for polite and professional responses.

Benefit: NLP-powered features make LinkedIn feel more intuitive, helping users communicate more effectively and discover content that resonates with their unique interests.

2. Machine Learning (ML)

LinkedIn's machine learning algorithms process massive amounts of data to improve user experiences. They analyze career trajectories, professional skills, and account activity to provide personalized insights that benefit job seekers and recruiters.

Example: LinkedIn's "People You May Know" feature is powered by ML, which predicts meaningful connections based on mutual connections, shared skills, and professional interests.

Benefit: ML makes job recommendations more accurate and ensures users build relevant and beneficial networks.

3. Predictive Analytics

Predictive analytics uses historical data and patterns to anticipate outcomes. LinkedIn's capability fuels features like job success rates, recruitment forecasts, and audience engagement insights.

Example: For job seekers, predictive analytics highlights profiles of users likely to match well with certain roles. Recruiters are given tools to predict hiring success for candidates based on specific job criteria.

Benefit: It saves time for both users and recruiters by enabling more intelligent decision-making and streamlining hiring processes.

4. AI-Generated Content Assistance

AI tools like Grammarly and LinkedIn's integrated content suggestions analyze the content users post. These tools help refine tone, grammar, and structure, ensuring professional and engaging communication.

Example: LinkedIn suggests phrases and completion prompts as users write headlines, summaries, or posts. These tools create concise, impactful content that captures the audience's attention.

Benefit: Users can enhance their professional image and increase content visibility without extensive writing expertise.

5. AI-Powered Video and Visual Processing

With video content's growing popularity, AI is helping LinkedIn users create engaging visual media. AI-powered tools suggest relevant video edits, captions, and taglines and optimize how visual content appears in feeds.

Example: LinkedIn uses AI to recommend shorter clip durations or add captions for improved accessibility and engagement with video content.

Benefit: Video creators can quickly produce professional-looking media that performs well on the platform.

Key Benefits for LinkedIn Users

AI technologies significantly heighten LinkedIn's value for professionals. Here are some of the top advantages:

1. Better Job Matching

AI-powered job recommendations consider your skills, preferences, and career history, ensuring you find opportunities you wouldn't otherwise come across.

2. Personalized Networking

Advanced analytics go beyond your first-degree connections, helping uncover meaningful links across industries based on shared interests or goals.

3. Enhanced Content Visibility

AI prioritizes relevant, high-quality posts in user feeds. Understanding content algorithms allows thought leaders to tailor their posts for greater exposure.

4. Time Savings for Recruitment

Recruiters save time with AI solutions that sieve through applications, recommend top candidates, and automate correspondence with qualified leads.

5. Actionable Insights

AI-powered analytics offer in-depth insights into what works for profiles, content, and outreach strategies. These insights ensure users continuously refine their approaches for maximum impact.

6. Improved Personal Branding

LinkedIn profiles optimized by AI suggestions stand out in a crowded professional landscape. Such profiles are more attractive to recruiters, collaborators, and audiences.

Challenges to Consider

Despite its offerings, emerging AI technologies on LinkedIn also come with challenges users must address:

1. Data Privacy Concerns

AI relies heavily on analyzing user data, leading to apprehension about how personal information is stored and used. Users must remain diligent about their privacy settings and usage agreements.

2. Bias in Algorithms

AI systems can unintentionally favor certain candidates, roles, or content types, creating bias. Users should stay aware of how these biases could impact their LinkedIn activity or visibility.

3. Adapting to New Features

The pace at which AI features are rolled out requires users to upskill frequently. Some professionals may find it challenging to adapt to sophisticated tools.

4. Over-Automation

While AI improves efficiency, over-reliance on automation risks diluting the human touch in networking and communication. Balancing automation with personal engagement is key.

Tips to Leverage Emerging AI Technologies on LinkedIn

Here's how you can make the most of AI tools for your LinkedIn presence:

1. Optimize Your Profile

Pay attention to AI-driven prompts for profile sections like your headline, summary, and skills list. Use relevant keywords that highlight your expertise for better visibility.

2. Engage with Personalized Insights

Leverage content curation tools to stay current on industry trends. Share thoughtful commentary on recommended posts to position yourself as a thought leader.

3. Refine Your Networking Strategy

Use LinkedIn's network recommendations and AI-powered messaging to build meaningful professional connections based on shared goals and mutual interests.

4. Use Content Analytics

Review analytics to understand which posts resonate most with your audience. Use this data to fine-tune your posting schedule and messaging style.

5. Participate in AI-Enhanced Job Searches

Job seekers should use "How You Match" features to close skill gaps. Tailor your applications using AI-driven feedback to address hiring needs directly.

6. Diversify Content Types

Experiment with AI tools to create videos, books, and posts to diversify your presence. Visual and multimedia formats often yield higher engagement.

7. Stay Updated on Privacy Practices

Understand and manage how your data is used within LinkedIn. Periodically update privacy settings to ensure you remain in control over your AI interactions.

In Conclusion

Emerging AI technologies are redefining LinkedIn's possibilities. By integrating natural language processing, predictive analytics, and machine learning, LinkedIn is creating a more personalized, efficient, and impactful platform for users at every stage of their professional journeys.

However, maximizing these advancements requires thoughtful engagement. Users must balance adaptation with a focus on authenticity, data privacy, and creativity. For anyone serious about standing out in their industry or finding new opportunities, learning how to leverage LinkedIn's AI capabilities is not just optional—it's essential. Align your strategy today with these technologies, and watch AI help unlock your next level of professional success.

Adapting Strategies to Evolving AI Capabilities

Artificial Intelligence (AI) is advancing at an unprecedented pace and becoming a driving force in modern industries. From reshaping customer experiences to optimizing operations, AI's influence is undeniable. For businesses, staying ahead in this AI-driven world requires more than acknowledging its potential—it demands strategic adaptability. Companies must rethink their approaches to innovation, operations, and workforce development to remain competitive and seize the opportunities AI presents.

This book explores how businesses can adapt to evolving AI capabilities, highlighting successful industry examples, key benefits, and the challenges organizations must overcome. We will also provide actionable tips to help your business build strategies that thrive in the era of AI.

Staying Agile in AI's Rapid Evolution

AI has evolved from a futuristic concept to tangible, game-changing technology in industries like healthcare, finance, and retail. Companies that adapt their strategies to AI advancements have experienced significant benefits, from reducing inefficiencies to revolutionizing customer interaction. However, continuous adaptation is crucial, as today's cutting-edge AI rapidly becomes tomorrow's standard.

1. Learning from Industry Successes

Several industries have embraced AI innovations and adapted their strategies to capitalize on its potential.

- **Healthcare**
  The healthcare sector has utilized AI to revolutionize diagnosis, treatment planning, and drug discovery. For example, AI-powered tools like IBM Watson Health analyze patient data to suggest

potential treatments. At the same time, image recognition AI detects anomalies in radiology scans faster and more accurately than humans. Hospitals and research institutions have improved patient outcomes and operational efficiency by integrating these capabilities into their workflows.

- **Finance**

  Financial services have incorporated AI-driven processes to manage risk, detect fraud, and offer personalized customer solutions. Automated trading algorithms and robo-advisors have become common, optimizing investments in real time. Companies like PayPal and JP Morgan Chase use AI to instantly detect fraudulent transactions, preventing large-scale financial risks more effectively than human monitoring alone.

- **Retail**

  Retailers like Amazon have leveraged AI to personalize shopping experiences through recommendation engines and predictive analytics. Virtual assistants, such as chatbots powered by natural language processing (NLP), make online shopping easier and more interactive. AI also enables dynamic pricing strategies that adjust based on demand, market conditions, and competitor behavior, helping retailers maximize revenue.

2. Benefits of Adapting to AI

Adopting and adapting to AI capabilities offers several significant advantages for businesses.

- **Enhanced Efficiency**

  AI automates mundane and repetitive tasks, freeing employees to focus on higher-value activities. For example, chatbots can instantly handle common queries in customer service, reducing wait times and increasing customer satisfaction.

- **Fostering Innovation**

  AI opens new possibilities for creating products and services, pushing industries toward groundbreaking advancements. Businesses that integrate AI early gain a head start in harnessing their creative potential.

- **Competitive Edge**

  Keeping up with AI ensures businesses stay ahead of competitors. Continuous adaptation to AI enables organizations to meet customer demands and anticipate future market trends proactively.

- **Data-Driven Decision Making**

  AI's ability to analyze mountains of data in real-time allows businesses to make informed decisions based on trends, patterns, and insights that might otherwise remain hidden.

Challenges of AI Adaptation

Adapting strategies to evolving AI presents its own set of challenges. Businesses must be prepared to address these obstacles to fully leverage AI's opportunities.

- **Continuous Learning Requirements**

  AI technologies are evolving so fast that staying up to date requires constant learning and reskilling of employees. Organizations must invest in ongoing education and training to remain current.

- **Ethical Concerns**

  With great power comes great responsibility. AI raises ethical considerations, including data privacy, transparency, and algorithmic bias. Failing to address these issues can result in reputational damage and regulatory scrutiny.

- **Potential Job Displacement**

  While AI enhances efficiency, it can also lead to workforce displacement in areas where automation outpaces the need for human labor. Businesses must balance their implementation of AI with a commitment to workforce reskilling and redeployment.

- **Implementation Costs**

  AI adoption often involves substantial initial investment in new software, systems, and training programs. For smaller businesses, the cost of implementation can be a significant barrier.

Tips for Adapting Business Strategies to AI

Adapting to AI advancements requires a combination of forward-thinking leadership, flexible planning, and a willingness to experiment. Here are actionable steps businesses can take to thrive amid AI's evolution:

1. Invest in AI Education and Training

Your workforce is your strongest asset when adapting to AI capabilities. Implement training programs focusing on AI literacy, equipping employees with the skills to work alongside AI tools and systems—partner with educational institutions or online learning platforms to facilitate skill development.

2. Foster a Culture of Innovation

Encourage employees at all levels to experiment with AI technologies and apply creative thinking. Create a safe space for testing new ideas, even if not all experiments succeed. Innovation thrives in environments where calculated risks are rewarded.

3. Implement Flexible Business Models

Capitalize on AI by adopting flexible and scalable business models. For instance, cloud computing solutions enable businesses to integrate AI with minimal disruption. Similarly, subscription-based or agile business approaches allow quick adjustments as AI evolves.

4. Monitor Industry Trends

Stay informed about AI advancements by attending industry events, subscribing to thought leader publications, and networking with AI experts. Understanding the direction AI is headed can help your business anticipate challenges and opportunities.

5. Prioritize Ethical AI Practices

Addressing ethical considerations isn't optional—it's strategic. Formulate clear guidelines on how AI will be implemented responsibly across your organization. Show transparency in how customer data is processed and used, and conduct regular audits to check for algorithmic biases.

6. Build Strong Partnerships

Collaborating with AI vendors, consultants, or technology partners can ease adaptation. Their specialized expertise can guide your business in identifying and implementing the most relevant AI technologies.

7. Start Small and Scale Strategically

Rather than overhauling entire systems simultaneously, test AI technologies with small, focused pilot projects. Once success is evident, scale those processes to other business areas. This allows for a smoother integration of AI without overwhelming your resources.

8. Communicate Transformation Goals

Transparent and frequent communication about AI adoption is essential for employee, stakeholder, and customer buy-in. Clearly articulate why AI is being implemented, what its goals are, and how it will benefit everyone involved.

In Conclusion

AI's rapid development shows no signs of slowing, and businesses must continuously evolve their strategies to keep pace. While the challenges of adapting can be daunting, the rewards—greater efficiency, innovation, and a competitive edge—far outweigh the risks.

The key to successful adaptation lies in a proactive and strategic approach. By investing in education, fostering a culture of innovation, and addressing ethical concerns, businesses can ride the wave of AI disruption and emerge stronger than ever. The future belongs to those willing to adapt; the time to act is now.

Predictions for the Future of AI on Professional Platforms

Artificial Intelligence (AI) is poised to reshape the future of professional platforms, drastically transforming how users network, collaborate, and pursue their career goals. Driven by advancements in machine learning, natural language processing, and predictive analytics, AI is expected to usher in a new era of efficiency and personalization across platforms like LinkedIn, Upwork, Freelancer, and more. These changes will impact the tools available to users and the underlying dynamics of professional development and hiring.

This book explores the potential advancements of AI on professional platforms, the benefits and challenges they bring, and how users can prepare to thrive in this automated, intelligent future.

The Evolution of AI Technologies in Professional Platforms

AI technologies continue to grow in sophistication, with potential breakthroughs on the horizon that could revolutionize professional platforms.

1. Advanced Machine Learning for Personalized User Experiences

Machine learning (ML) has already made its mark on platforms like LinkedIn through features such as personalized job recommendations and connection suggestions. However, the future could see ML models becoming more intuitive and granular. An AI-powered platform might analyze your career history and subtler factors, such as performance reviews or social media activity, to offer even more precise recommendations for job opportunities, training, and potential collaborators.

ML could improve the matchmaking process between employers and freelancers for freelance platforms like Upwork. For instance, algorithms trained on successful past projects could predict compatibility and increase the likelihood of fruitful partnerships.

2. Natural Language Processing for Seamless Communication

Natural language processing (NLP) will likely advance to provide enhanced communication and content generation tools. Imagine AI that can assist with crafting professional messages, proposals, or even entire project pitches in real-time while aligning with the recipient's tone and preferences. Furthermore, NLP could help break language barriers by providing instant and accurate translations, fostering global collaboration regardless of one's native tongue.

Additionally, AI-driven sentiment analysis could help users understand the tone of job postings, company reviews, or client interactions, ensuring more informed decision-making when pursuing opportunities.

3. Predictive Analytics for Career Path Navigation

Predictive analytics is already being used on professional platforms to predict job success and forecast trends. Looking ahead, AI tools may better predict industry trends and emerging skills tied to those trends. For example, LinkedIn users might get insights into upcoming in-demand roles and receive suggestions for relevant skill development courses or certifications.

Similar predictive insights could benefit freelancers, such as forecasts about the most sought-after services in their domain or optimal bidding strategies to secure high-value contracts.

4. AI for Continuous Skill Development

AI could also transform the way users build their skills. Professional platforms may integrate learning systems powered by adaptive AI, which can analyze a user's strengths, weaknesses, and preferred learning formats to create bespoke educational paths. These systems could also evaluate users' capabilities through project simulations, awarding skill certifications based on performance rather than just course completion.

Upwork or Freelancer could use AI to help freelancers continuously enhance their skills through task-specific microlearning modules, making staying competitive in the gig economy easier.

5. Virtual Advisors and Career Coaches

Imagine having an AI-driven mentor built right into your favorite professional platform. These virtual advisors would combine insights from machine learning, NLP, and predictive analytics to guide users' career journeys. From suggesting the best networking strategies to identifying blind spots in a user's professional profile, these AI tools could serve as personalized coaches that guide decision-making and ensure growth.

6. Immersive AI Experiences with AR and VR

Augmented reality (AR) and virtual reality (VR), enhanced by AI, could take professional interactions to a new level. Platforms might introduce virtual career fairs, conferences, or one-on-one networking opportunities in immersive 3D environments, making geographic and time constraints less relevant. AI could act as a facilitator in these spaces, curating experiences and recommending conversation starters based on participants' profiles.

The Benefits of AI Advancements on Professional Platforms

The evolution of AI on professional platforms brings various benefits for users across industries and roles.

1. Personalized Career Journeys

AI technologies will help professionals navigate their path by offering tailored guidance on job opportunities, relevant skill development, and networking strategies.

2. Improved Efficiency

AI automation will streamline time-consuming tasks like writing proposals, filtering job postings, and scheduling interviews. This allows users to concentrate on building relationships and tasks that truly matter.

3. Enhanced Networking

AI will make networking more relevant and impactful by recommending connections that align with shared interests, goals, or complementary profiles, helping users quickly expand the right type of professional relationships.

4. Global Collaboration Opportunities

By breaking language and cultural barriers, AI-driven tools will encourage seamless collaboration for users across the globe, fostering a truly interconnected workforce.

5. Greater Job Market Access

Through predictive analytics and real-time insights, professionals will have access to emerging job markets, helping them stay ahead of industry trends and secure opportunities in evolving fields.

Challenges of AI in Professional Platforms

While the future of AI is exciting, it isn't without its complications. Businesses and professionals alike need to prepare for the challenges associated with these advancements.

1. Data Privacy

AI relies heavily on collecting and analyzing data to make predictions and offer recommendations. However, the misuse or mishandling of user data remains a serious concern. Professionals will need reassurance that their data is managed ethically and securely.

2. Ethical Concerns

AI algorithms can potentially introduce or reinforce biases in hiring, promotion, or ranking systems. Transparent algorithm design and ethical guidelines will be critical in minimizing these risks.

3. Impact on Human Interaction

While AI accelerates automation, there's a risk of losing the human touch that many professional interactions require, such as tailored mentoring or emotional support during job transitions. Striking a balance between automation and authenticity remains a key challenge.

4. Need for Continuous Adaptation

Professionals will need to constantly learn new skills and technologies to keep up with the rapid evolution of AI, potentially creating stress or challenges for those who struggle with digital transformation.

Preparing for the AI-Driven Future of Professional Platforms

Users should take proactive steps to adapt and grow alongside these technologies to stay competitive in an AI-enhanced professional world.

1. Stay Updated on AI Trends

Follow thought leaders, attend webinars, and subscribe to relevant publications to remain informed about the latest AI developments and their potential impact on professional platforms.

2. Build Digital and AI Literacy

Understand how AI works and familiarize yourself with the tools unique to your field. For example, learn to utilize AI-powered analysis tools or improve communication using NLP-generated tips.

3. Enhance Soft Skills

Traditional skills like empathy and critical thinking—the "human" elements of professional interaction—will remain crucial. These skills complement AI technologies and ensure you stand out in an automated environment.

4. Develop Agility

Adaptability will become one of the most sought-after traits. Be willing to experiment with new technologies and pivot strategies to stay relevant in a constantly changing landscape.

5. Engage Actively with AI Tools

Instead of passively using AI tools, actively explore how they can bring you closer to your goals. Use AI-generated recommendations as prompts, not rigid rules, to shape your unique approach.

In Conclusion

The future of AI on professional platforms promises exciting opportunities for professionals seeking to advance their careers, enhance their skills, and expand their networks. From AI-driven insights that make career decisions easier to tools that facilitate global collaboration, the potential of this technology is boundless.

However, users must engage thoughtfully with these advancements and prepare themselves for a constantly evolving professional landscape. By staying informed, developing adaptive skills, and balancing the advantages of automation with the need for human connection, professionals can thrive in this AI-powered future. The revolution is coming—are you ready to lead it?

Chapter 9

The Ethics of AI on LinkedIn

Artificial Intelligence (AI) has become an integral part of LinkedIn, driving its ability to connect professionals, recommend jobs, and personalize user experiences. However, as AI evolves, it also raises various ethical concerns that impact the platform's users and integrity. With over 900 million members worldwide, LinkedIn is responsible for upholding trust and fairness through ethical AI practices. Yet, maintaining this balance is far from simple, especially given the complexities of data usage, algorithmic transparency, and potential biases.

This chapter dives into the ethical considerations surrounding AI on LinkedIn, provides real-world examples of challenges and solutions, and offers actionable recommendations for fostering ethical AI use on professional networking platforms.

The Role of AI on LinkedIn

AI underpins much of LinkedIn's effectiveness and engagement. From suggesting connections and job postings to generating insights on user activity, LinkedIn's AI models analyze enormous amounts of data to deliver value to its users. For instance, the "People You May Know" feature uses machine learning algorithms to predict potential connections, while its job recommendation system evaluates users' profiles, skills, and career histories to propose suitable opportunities.

While these tools enhance user experiences and make networking more efficient, they raise critical ethical questions about how data is collected, processed, and applied. The features that provide value can also pose risks if not handled responsibly.

Ethical Considerations with AI on LinkedIn

To fully grasp the ethical implications of AI on LinkedIn, it is essential to explore three key issues that impact users and the platform alike:

1. Data Privacy

LinkedIn relies on vast amounts of user data to power its AI algorithms. This includes information users willingly provide, such as job titles and skills, as well as behavioral data, including profile visits, clicks, and connections formed. While this data enables LinkedIn to offer personalized services, questions about the security and handling of that data arise.

For example, do users fully understand how their data is collected and used? Are they aware of how LinkedIn might share data with third parties for insights or advertising purposes? Concerns over data breaches and unauthorized sharing loom, threatening user trust and platform integrity.

2. Algorithmic Bias

AI models are only as unbiased as the data they are trained on, and LinkedIn's algorithms are no exception. If the training data includes existing biases—such as underrepresentation of certain genders or ethnicities—it can perpetuate and even amplify those biases.

For instance, LinkedIn's job recommendation feature might disproportionately show high-paying roles to male users if the underlying data reflects historical gender imbalances in certain industries. This could unintentionally limit opportunities for female users and perpetuate inequality. Biases in algorithms harm not only individuals but also LinkedIn's reputation by undermining its commitment to fairness and diversity.

3. Transparency

Transparency refers to how openly LinkedIn communicates about how its AI systems operate. Many users lack a clear understanding of how recommendations, rankings, or visibility works on the platform. For example, why do certain profiles appear for recruiters while others do not? Why do some posts gain more visibility than others?

Users may feel disconnected from LinkedIn's processes without clear explanations, fostering suspicion and mistrust. Transparency is foundational to maintaining ethical AI use and ensuring users feel empowered and informed.

Ethical Challenges LinkedIn Faces and Response Efforts

Ethical AI challenges are complex and multifaceted, but LinkedIn has taken steps to address these issues. Below are a few examples:

1. Addressing Data Privacy Concerns

LinkedIn has adopted policies to give users more control over their data. Privacy settings allow members to manage aspects like how their profile appears in search results and whether their data is used for targeted advertisements. Additionally, LinkedIn complies with regulations such as the General Data Protection Regulation (GDPR) in Europe, which mandates transparency about data collection and the right to delete personal information.

While these steps are commendable, critics argue that privacy policies are often too long or complex for most users to understand fully. Simplifying these terms and making them more transparent could further improve trust.

2. Battling Algorithmic Bias

LinkedIn has implemented fairness initiatives in its hiring systems to minimize bias. For example, its Recruiter tool now anonymizes candidate names and photos to reduce implicit bias among hiring managers. Furthermore, LinkedIn's AI teams conduct reviews and audits of algorithms to identify and correct unintended biases.

However, achieving true algorithmic fairness remains an ongoing challenge. It requires regular updates to models, diverse datasets, and increased collaboration with independent researchers who can offer unbiased evaluations.

3. Improving transparency

LinkedIn has begun providing insights into its algorithms and ranking systems. For example, the platform has introduced tools that explain how job matches are determined or why certain posts gain prominence in user feeds. Additionally, LinkedIn publishes ethical AI principles that outline its approach to fairness, privacy, and accountability.

Still, greater transparency is needed, especially regarding how AI prioritizes content and connections. More user-friendly resources like videos or interactive guides could help bridge this gap.

Recommendations for Ethical AI Use on LinkedIn

Promoting ethical AI on LinkedIn requires joint efforts from the platform's developers, its users, and the broader tech community. Here are some actionable recommendations:

For LinkedIn:

1. **Regular Audits of AI Systems**
   Conduct routine, independent audits of algorithms to identify biases and assess compliance with fairness guidelines. Make the results of these audits available to the public.

2. **Enhance User-Friendly Transparency**
   Replace opaque technical jargon with plain language explanations about how LinkedIn's AI systems operate. Provide clear visuals or

simulations that demystify processes like ranking and recommendation.

3. **Ethical Training for Developers**

Provide ongoing ethical development training for LinkedIn's AI engineers and data scientists. Equip them with the tools to anticipate ethical dilemmas and mitigate harm proactively.

4. **Diversify Input Data**

Ensure that datasets used to train AI models represent various users regarding gender, ethnicity, geography, and industry, reducing the risks of perpetuating existing imbalances.

For Users:

1. **Learn About Data Rights**

Please educate yourself about the data you share on LinkedIn and how it is used. Use privacy settings and review the platform's terms of service to ensure you retain control over your information.

2. **Advocate for Inclusive Algorithms**

Engage with LinkedIn by providing feedback on features or tools that feel exclusionary or biased. Public discourse and user insights play a vital role in holding companies accountable.

3. **Leverage Platform Transparency Tools**

Use LinkedIn's tools and dashboards to explain post visibility or job match predictions. Understanding these systems better can help you optimize your profile and activity.

4. **Support Ethical AI Practices**

Amplify discussions about fairness, inclusivity, and privacy on professional networking platforms. By raising awareness, you contribute to a collective push for ethical improvements.

In Conclusion

Ethical AI on LinkedIn is not just about improving algorithms—it's about safeguarding user trust, fostering equality, and ensuring AI serves everyone equitably. While LinkedIn has made strides in addressing concerns around data privacy, algorithmic bias, and transparency, much work still needs to be done. Users, developers, and organizations must engage in ongoing dialogue and take shared responsibility to ensure the platform remains a space for fair and meaningful connections.

By promoting ethical practices, LinkedIn can continue to empower its members, connecting them to the right opportunities while maintaining the integrity of its AI-driven ecosystem. For professionals, understanding these ethical dimensions is vital for navigating LinkedIn effectively and championing a more responsible approach to AI in all corners of the professional world.

Balancing Automation and Authenticity

Automation has revolutionized how we work, interact, and conduct business, offering unprecedented efficiency and scalability. From chatbots resolving customer inquiries in seconds to AI-driven tools streamlining recruitment, automation has become a powerful force across industries. However, as businesses and professionals increasingly rely on automation, a critical question arises—how do we maintain authenticity in our interactions?

Authenticity fosters trust, credibility, and meaningful connections, vital for long-term success. Striking the right balance between automation and the personal touch can be a challenge, but it's necessary to ensure that the human element isn't overshadowed by technology. This book explores how businesses and professionals can achieve this balance, highlighting especially critical industries and providing actionable strategies for success.

The Role of Automation in Professional Settings

Automation technology, powered by AI and machine learning, has proven valuable across various industries. It can perform repetitive tasks, analyze vast amounts of data, and even accurately predict outcomes. Its benefits are undeniable—faster operations, cost savings, and improved scalability. For example:

- **Customer Service:** Chatbots and virtual assistants handle routine inquiries 24/7, providing customers quick responses and freeing support teams to focus on complex cases.
- **Marketing:** Email automation tools deliver personalized campaigns at scale, ensuring timely and relevant communication without requiring manual input for every interaction.
- **Human Resources:** Automated applicant tracking systems (ATS) streamline the hiring process, enabling recruiters to review resumes and identify top candidates more efficiently.

Despite these advantages, over-relying on automation risks making interactions feel impersonal and disconnected. There's no substitute for the empathy and understanding only humans can offer.

Challenges of Balancing Automation and Authenticity

Achieving harmony between automation and personal connection poses several challenges, including the following:

1. Over-automation leading to Impersonal Experiences

Relying too much on automation can create interactions that feel sterile or robotic. For instance, generic email responses or chatbot errors can make customers feel undervalued. While automation excels at routine tasks, it often struggles to replicate the nuance and responsiveness of a skilled human.

2. The Perception of Losing the Human Touch

Automation risks alienating clients, employees, or customers if it replaces too many human functions. Feelings of being "just another number" can hurt loyalty and trust, especially during high-stakes or emotionally sensitive situations.

3. Integrating Automation Seamlessly

Many organizations struggle to integrate automation to complement human efforts rather than replacing or overshadowing them. Fumbling this integration can lead to disjointed and frustrating processes for the end user.

4. Understanding When Automation is Appropriate

Automation isn't a one-size-fits-all solution. Over-automating certain areas while neglecting others can create inconsistencies. Knowing when and where to apply automation requires careful judgment and foresight.

Industries Where Balance Is Crucial

Striking the right balance between automation and authenticity is vital in industries where relationships and trust are key to success.

1. Customer Service

Excellent customer service depends on empathy and personalization. While chatbots effectively handle FAQs or minor concerns, they cannot provide emotional support to resolve complex or sensitive issues. For example, an airline can use bots to manage rebooking during a flight delay, but passengers experiencing heightened frustration may still require a compassionate human representative.

2. Marketing

Marketing automation enables businesses to send targeted messages and nurture leads efficiently. However, inauthentic or overly generic marketing campaigns can alienate audiences. Striking the balance means tailoring messages using customer data while still projecting a business's unique voice and values. A good example is personalized video messages that leverage automation to include customer names but retain a human tone.

3. Human Resources

HR leaders use automation to identify top candidates quickly, but people want genuine engagement during recruitment. Receiving cold, automated rejection emails without personalized feedback can leave candidates with a negative impression of a company. Balancing efficiency with thoughtful human interaction ensures applicants feel respected throughout the process.

4. Healthcare

AI tools analyze patient data to recommend treatments or detect potential health issues, saving time. However, clinicians must pair these insights with compassionate communication to ensure patients feel heard and cared for. Balance requires combining AI's diagnostic power with a doctor's personal touch.

Strategies for Balancing Automation and Authenticity

Maintaining authenticity in an increasingly automated world means taking care when designing customer journeys or professional interactions. Below are actionable strategies to strike the perfect balance:

1. Reserve Automation for Routine or Repetitive Tasks

Automation works best when applied to tasks that don't require creativity, empathy, or decision-making. Free your people from mundane workflows, such as data entry, so that they can devote their energy to more high-impact activities. For example, scheduling software can be used to book appointments but ensure a human receptionist is on hand to greet clients warmly.

2. Invest in Training for AI Systems and Teams

Ensuring that automation systems integrate smoothly with human effort is essential. Train your team to manage automated tools effectively and involve them in identifying gaps where personal interaction is needed.

3. Humanize Automated Interactions

Where possible, inject some personality into your automated systems. For example, design chatbot conversations that match your brand's tone—professional yet approachable. Small touches like this can make automation feel personable instead of purely functional.

4. Use Automation to Facilitate (Not Replace) Personalization

Automation enables businesses to handle customer data on a massive scale, but crafting personalized experiences is where it truly shines. For instance, email marketing tools can segment audiences and create tailored messages, yet the language and messaging should still resonate authentically. Customers should feel like they're engaging with a real person, even when automation is involved.

5. Prioritize High-Value Human Interaction

Devote human effort to situations that demand empathy, critical thinking, or nuanced responses. For example, in customer service, ensure representatives intervene during escalated issues or moments of emotional distress. Personal touch in these areas can significantly enhance trust and loyalty.

6. Gather and Act on Feedback

Regularly solicit feedback from your customers, employees, or audience to understand how your automation efforts are perceived. Use this data to improve systems while ensuring human engagement meets evolving expectations.

7. Combine Technology with Emotional Intelligence

Teach your team to leverage technology while staying mindful of the importance of empathy, compassion, and cultural sensitivity. Even as automation advances, emotional intelligence will remain a uniquely human strength.

8. Be Transparent

Honesty about when and where automation is being used helps manage expectations and humanize interactions. For example, letting customers know they're chatting with a bot instead of pretending it's a real person creates transparency and builds trust.

Benefits of Balancing Automation and Authenticity

Businesses can enjoy the best of both worlds when they strike the right balance. Benefits include:

- **Efficiency Without Compromising Trust**
  Automation streamlines operations while maintaining integrity and warmth to earn customer or employee loyalty.

- **Enhanced Brand Perception**

  An effective balance is often reflected in how audiences view a business. Customers appreciate businesses that value time-saving tools yet remain approachable and genuine.

- **Improved Employee Satisfaction**

  Relieving employees of repetitive tasks through automation allows them to focus on fulfilling human-centric roles, boosting overall morale.

- **Stronger Relationships**

  Personalized interactions, supported by automation insights, can deepen relationships with clients, employees, and stakeholders.

In Conclusion

Balancing automation and authenticity isn't just a strategic necessity—it's an art form that demands thoughtfulness, creativity, and constant refinement. The key lies in automating with intention, allowing technology to elevate efficiency while ensuring the personal touch remains at the center of human interactions.

Businesses and individuals can build trust, foster genuine connections, and thrive in an increasingly automated world by using automation as a tool to amplify rather than replace humanity. After all, the future may be digital, but the heart of every meaningful interaction will always be distinctly human.

Understanding Privacy Concerns with AI and Data Collection

Artificial Intelligence (AI) has rapidly transformed how we live and work, delivering remarkable benefits across industries. From personalized recommendations on streaming platforms to advanced diagnostics in healthcare, AI's ability to collect, process, and analyze massive amounts of data has revolutionized nearly every sector. However, this growing dependence on AI also brings significant privacy concerns to the forefront, particularly regarding how personal data is collected, managed, and utilized.

Understanding these privacy issues is no longer optional for individuals and businesses alike—it's essential. This book examines the growing concerns surrounding AI and data collection, their implications, and how they impact individuals and industries. Additionally, it explores regulations and best practices, offering strategies for safeguarding privacy in an increasingly AI-driven world.

How AI Collects and Uses Data

AI systems rely on large datasets to function effectively. They require access to personal, behavioral, and transactional data to train machine learning models or power algorithms. Here's how AI typically collects and uses data:

- **Behavioral Analysis**

  Search histories, click patterns, and location data are regularly collected to gain insights into users' preferences. For instance, e-commerce platforms use this information to recommend products tailored to individual tastes.

- **Biometric Data**

  AI systems in industries like healthcare or security collect sensitive data, such as fingerprints, facial scans, or genetic information, for authentication and diagnostic purposes.

- **Social Media Activity**

  Most major platforms use AI to analyze user content, likes, and connections, feeding algorithms responsible for serving personalized feeds and targeted ads.

- **Predictive Analytics**

   AI models use historical data, such as purchasing behavior or financial records, to predict future trends, enabling businesses to deliver personalized offers or improve decision-making.

While these applications bring convenience and innovation, they also raise concerns about how far-reaching and invasive data collection practices have become.

Privacy Concerns with AI and Data Collection

The vast scale of data collection by AI systems has created several potential risks for both individuals and businesses. These risks often arise from the interplay of advanced technology and inadequate safeguards.

1. Data Breaches and Security Risks

The accumulation of sensitive data in centralized systems makes it an attractive target for cyberattacks. A single data breach can expose millions of individuals' information. For example, the healthcare industry, which uses AI for patient diagnosis and management, has experienced major breaches that leaked medical records, compromising patients' privacy.

2. Misuse or Exploitation of Personal Information

Personal data collected by AI systems may be used for purposes users never agreed to. Social media scandals, such as the misuse of user data for political profiling, highlight how personal information can be weaponized without consent. AI's ability to analyze and manipulate behavioral patterns raises concerns about ethical boundaries and exploitation.

3. Lack of Transparency and Control

AI algorithms are often referred to as "black boxes" because they operate in ways that are not easily explained or understood by everyday users. People often don't know what data is being collected, how it's processed, and how the outcomes affect them. This lack of transparency leaves users feeling powerless over their own information.

4. Over-Collection of Data

Many systems collect and store data beyond what is strictly necessary for their intended function. For instance, mobile apps often request permissions that have little relevance to their operations, such as access to contacts or location data.

5. Erosion of Privacy in Everyday Life

AI's pervasiveness means privacy issues are no longer confined to specific interactions. Connected devices, such as smart speakers and wearable tech, constantly monitor behaviors, contributing to the erosion of personal boundaries. This near-constant surveillance creates an environment where privacy becomes nearly impossible.

Industries Impacted by Privacy Concerns

While all sectors using AI face privacy challenges, some industries are disproportionately affected by these concerns due to the sensitive nature of the data they handle.

1. Healthcare

AI has pushed the boundaries of diagnostic accuracy and patient care, but it has also amplified risks concerning medical records, genetic data, and patient histories. Many hospitals and health tech companies struggle to protect this extremely sensitive data from external breaches.

2. Finance

Banks and financial firms use AI to detect fraud, assess creditworthiness, and optimize investment strategies. However, stolen financial records from data breaches harm individuals and undermine trust in financial institutions.

3. Social Media

Perhaps the most visible arena for privacy debates, social media platforms are notorious for harvesting vast quantities of user data to refine advertising algorithms. The unauthorized use of personal data by third-party applications has sparked international outrage and demands for regulation.

4. Retail and E-Commerce

AI's ability to track consumer behavior has revolutionized retail, allowing businesses to deliver hyper-personalized offers. However, the extensive profiling of consumers creates vulnerabilities, as data can be shared, sold, or compromised without their knowledge.

Current Regulations and Best Practices

To combat privacy concerns, governments and organizations have introduced regulations and best practices to protect personal information in an AI-driven world.

1. The General Data Protection Regulation (GDPR)

Implemented by the European Union, GDPR is one of the most comprehensive privacy laws in the world. It requires organizations to clearly state how user data is collected and used, obtain explicit consent, and allow individuals control over their information.

2. The California Consumer Privacy Act (CCPA)

CCPA provides California residents with the right to know what personal data companies collect, the ability to opt out of data sales, and assurances that their data will not be used negligently. It has set a precedent for similar regulations in the U.S.

3. Encryption and Anonymization

Many organizations now utilize encryption to secure data in transit and storage, ensuring that the stolen data remains indecipherable even if breaches occur. Anonymizing personally identifiable data is another approach that minimizes privacy risks.

4. AI Audits

Regular reviews of AI models and datasets ensure fairness, transparency, and compliance with privacy norms. These audits help detect unethical practices in data collection or algorithmic design.

Strategies to Safeguard Privacy

Both individuals and organizations have roles to play in ensuring that privacy is protected in the age of AI.

For Individuals:

1. **Understand Data Rights**
   Learn about privacy policies and understand your rights under regulations like GDPR or CCPA. Use tools provided by platforms to manage your data permissions.

2. **Be Cautious About Sharing Data**
   Limit the amount of personal information you share online. Review app permissions regularly and restrict access to unnecessary data points like location tracking.

3. **Use Privacy Tools**

   Leverage privacy-focused tools such as VPNs, encrypted messaging apps, and ad blockers to maintain control over your data.

4. **Advocate for Transparency**

   Push for clearer communication from businesses about their data collection practices. Being an informed consumer can help encourage more ethical behaviors.

For Businesses:

1. **Adopt Privacy-First Design Principles**

   Build systems that prioritize user consent and minimize the collection of unnecessary data. Transparency at the design stage fosters trust.

2. **Invest in Cybersecurity**

   Implement advanced encryption methods, two-factor authentication, and routine penetration testing to strengthen your organization's defenses against data breaches.

3. **Comply with Regulations**

   Ensure alignment with local and international regulations such as GDPR and CCPA. Non-compliance not only damages your reputation but can also result in hefty fines.

4. **Conduct Regular Privacy Audits**

   Regularly evaluate AI tools and data management practices to identify and mitigate risks. Engage external experts for unbiased assessments where needed.

In Conclusion

AI and data collection are undeniably intertwined with innovation, efficiency, and economic growth. However, their privacy concerns are equally significant and must be addressed to build a system that serves all stakeholders ethically and responsibly.

Individuals and businesses can thrive in the AI era without compromising trust by understanding privacy risks, advocating for transparent practices, and actively safeguarding personal data. Amid rapid technological change, protecting privacy isn't just a matter of compliance—it's a key to sustaining long-term success in our increasingly interconnected world.

Mitigating Risks of Over-Reliance on AI Tools

Artificial Intelligence (AI) has become a critical tool across multiple sectors, driving efficiencies, improving decision-making, and enabling innovations at an unprecedented scale. AI is increasingly embedded in our daily lives, from diagnosing diseases in healthcare to automating financial transactions and personalizing educational experiences. Its capabilities are undeniably impressive, but there is a growing need to address the risks of over-relying on these advanced technologies.

When organizations and individuals put excessive trust in AI, the consequences can be significant, often leading to errors, ethical dilemmas, and a breakdown of critical human oversight. Striking a balance between leveraging AI's potential and maintaining human judgment is essential to unlocking its full benefits responsibly. This book will explore the dangers of AI over-reliance, offer examples of real-world incidents, and provide actionable strategies to mitigate these risks.

Understanding the Risks of Over-Reliance on AI

The increasing popularity of AI tools in areas like healthcare, finance, and education has brought undeniable advantages. However, over-reliance on these automated systems can introduce vulnerabilities that may lead to unintended and harmful outcomes. Below are some key risks associated with excessive dependence on AI technologies:

1. Loss of Human Oversight

AI systems are designed to automate decision-making processes, but removing human involvement entirely can have serious consequences. Blind faith in a system's recommendations or outputs often leads to missed opportunities for critical evaluation. For example, if medical professionals rely solely on AI to analyze test results, they may overlook important anomalies the system was not trained to detect.

2. AI Errors and Bias

AI technologies are inherently dependent on the data on which they are trained. Poorly curated datasets or unintentional biases in training data can result in inaccurate predictions or discriminatory outcomes. For instance, AI algorithms used in hiring have been found to prefer male candidates over female ones due to biased input data reflecting existing workplace inequalities.

3. Ethical Concerns

Over-reliance on AI raises ethical challenges, particularly around accountability. Who is responsible when AI makes the wrong call—those who designed it or those who implemented it? This lack of clarity becomes especially problematic in sensitive areas like criminal justice, finance, or healthcare.

4. Erosion of Human Skills

Relying too heavily on AI can erode essential human skills over time. For example, AI tutoring systems in education may undermine teachers' ability to engage students effectively. Similarly, professionals may lose critical thinking skills if they default to AI-generated solutions without question.

5. Systemic Vulnerabilities

AI's heavy integration into various systems creates potential single points of failure. If an AI system crashes or is compromised, essential processes can halt. For instance, a malfunctioning trading algorithm in finance could lead to massive market disruptions.

6. Overconfidence in AI's Scope

AI tools excel in specific tasks but are not universally capable. Over-relying on their capabilities without understanding their limitations can cause major errors. For example, AI may be great at identifying patterns in data but may lack the intuition required for creative problem-solving or ethical decision-making.

Real-World Examples of AI Over-Reliance

Several incidents provide stark reminders of the risks involved with depending too much on AI technologies:

- **Healthcare:** IBM's Watson for Oncology was designed to recommend cancer treatments but was found sometimes to suggest unsafe options. The recommendations stemmed from a lack of clinical data diversity during training, highlighting the risks of unquestioning trust in AI tools for life-critical decisions.
- **Finance:** The 2010 Flash Crash in the U.S. stock market was triggered by automated trading algorithms operating at high speeds. The over-reliance on AI-driven strategies caused unprecedented market volatility, wiping out hundreds of billions of dollars in minutes before the markets stabilized.

- **Criminal Justice:** Predictive policing algorithms designed to identify crime-prone areas were found to perpetuate racial biases due to flawed training data. Over-reliance on these tools led to over-policing of minority neighborhoods, raising serious ethical concerns.
- **Navigation Systems:** Reliance on GPS systems has occasionally led drivers astray, including incidents where vehicles were directed onto dangerous, impassable roads or into restricted areas. Blind faith in AI-powered GPS systems can replace basic human judgment, resulting in accidents or mishaps.

Strategies to Mitigate AI Over-Reliance

To prevent these risks, organizations and individuals must adopt thoughtful strategies that ensure AI tools complement, rather than replace, human capabilities. Below are key measures to address over-reliance on AI:

1. Maintain Human Oversight

AI should augment human decision-making, not replace it. Establish protocols that ensure human involvement in critical decisions, especially in high-risk industries like healthcare, finance, and law enforcement. For example, doctors can use AI for diagnostic support but must validate any recommendations before delivering treatment.

2. Implement Rigorous Testing and Validation

Organizations must routinely test AI tools to ensure they function accurately and ethically. Validation processes should involve diverse data inputs to identify and eliminate hidden biases or faulty outputs. Continuous testing is critical as AI systems adapt and change over time.

3. Foster Human-AI Collaboration

Encourage the use of AI as a collaborative tool that enhances human capabilities. For example, in education, teachers can use AI software to analyze students' progress while still playing an active role in shaping individual learning experiences.

4. Invest in Training and Education

Both developers and end-users of AI tools must be well-trained to understand the technology's limitations and potential pitfalls. Training programs focused on AI ethics, data analysis, and critical evaluation can help users maintain vigilance and responsibility when using automated tools.

5. Prioritize transparency

AI systems should be designed with explainability, enabling users to understand how decisions or recommendations are made. Transparency helps build trust and allows users to identify when errors occur. For instance, providing insight into how an AI recruitment system scores job candidates can reveal flaws that might go unnoticed.

6. Implement Fail-Safe Measures

Design AI tools with fail-safes to manage errors or malfunctions. For example, financial trading algorithms should be programmed to halt automatically during significant market irregularities, reducing the chances of catastrophic failures.

7. Encourage a Culture of Continuous Learning

AI systems and the professionals who use them must constantly adapt to changing conditions, new data, and emerging risks. Businesses should support a culture prioritizing learning and innovation, empowering teams to question AI outputs, audit systems, and explore alternative approaches.

8. Balance Automation with Human Touch

While automation improves efficiency, a human element is necessary for empathy, creativity, and nuanced decision-making. A healthcare provider, for instance, should combine AI-driven diagnostic tools with the interpersonal skills required to support and reassure patients.

In Conclusion

AI tools are powerful enablers of progress, but they are not infallible. Organizations and individuals must approach these systems with a healthy balance of enthusiasm and skepticism, ensuring that automation supports—not substitutes—human expertise. By adopting targeted strategies such as maintaining oversight, rigorous testing, and fostering collaboration, we can harness AI's potential without succumbing to its risks.

Ultimately, the smartest systems in the world cannot replace humans' critical thinking, creativity, and ethical considerations. Striking this balance is not just a strategic necessity but a moral imperative for responsible innovation in an increasingly AI-driven world.

Building Trust and Credibility in an AI-Driven World

Artificial Intelligence (AI) has become a transformative force, reshaping industries and daily life through innovation and efficiency. AI systems now influence crucial areas like healthcare, finance, transportation, and communication. However, building trust and credibility in these systems is increasingly important as AI becomes more embedded in society. Without these pillars, users may hesitate to adopt innovations, and businesses risk facing reputational damage or regulatory scrutiny.

It is undeniable that trust is fragile in the context of AI, given concerns about transparency, accountability, and ethical usage. This book examines the challenges to building trust in AI, provides examples of industries where trust is paramount, and outlines actionable strategies for earning and maintaining credibility with stakeholders in an AI-driven future.

The Critical Role of Trust in AI

Trust is central to the successful integration of AI into society. Users and stakeholders need confidence that AI systems are accurate, fair, secure, and aligned with their best interests. Without this trust, adoption slows, and potential benefits are out of reach.

Building credibility goes beyond relying on innovative technology—it requires demonstrating reliability, ethical practices, and clear communication at every stage of AI development and deployment. When done right, trust can foster user engagement, boost return on investment, and pave the way for seamless collaboration between humans and machines.

Challenges to Building Trust in AI

Creating AI systems that inspire trust and credibility is no small feat. Several challenges stand in the way of achieving this goal in an AI-driven world:

1. Transparency and Explainability

AI systems are often described as "black boxes" because their inner workings are complex and difficult to understand. Users may not comprehend how a decision was made, why an algorithm behaved a certain way, or what data was used for training. This lack of transparency erodes trust, especially in high-stakes scenarios like loan approvals or criminal sentencing.

2. Accountability and Responsibility

Who is to blame when AI systems fail? Whether it's a biased hiring algorithm or a malfunctioning autonomous vehicle, determining accountability can be tricky. Ambiguities around responsibility— whether it lies with AI creators, businesses, or end-users—undermine credibility and make trust harder to establish.

3. Ethical Concerns

Unethical uses of AI, such as surveillance without consent, algorithmic discrimination, or manipulation of public opinion, create skepticism. Cases, where AI systems violate human rights or exacerbate existing inequalities, demonstrate the ethical minefield businesses must navigate to maintain trust.

4. Security and Data Privacy

AI requires vast amounts of data, often including sensitive personal information. Concerns about how data is collected, stored, and utilized—especially in light of high-profile breaches—further diminish user confidence.

5. Bias and Fairness

AI systems trained on unrepresentative or biased data may produce discriminatory or unjust outcomes. For example, facial recognition software has been shown to perform poorly for certain ethnic groups due to insufficient or biased training datasets. Addressing these biases is crucial for equitable outcomes, yet it requires intentional effort and rigorous design processes.

Industries Where Trust is Crucial

Trust plays a critical role in all sectors touched by AI, but it is particularly vital in industries where decisions directly affect people's lives and livelihoods.

1. Healthcare

AI applications in healthcare include diagnostic tools, treatment recommendations, and patient monitoring. For patients and providers to trust these systems, they must be reliable, explainable, and proven to improve outcomes. Ethical concerns, like ensuring patient confidentiality or avoiding biased treatment algorithms, make trust-building even more critical in this industry.

2. Finance

AI powers fraud detection, credit scoring, and algorithmic trading. Mistakes can have significant financial consequences for individuals and institutions alike. Transparency in decision-making processes, such as explaining why a loan application was denied, is essential for earning users' trust in financial AI tools.

3. Autonomous Vehicles

Self-driving cars rely on AI to make split-second decisions about navigation and safety. Building trust among passengers, pedestrians, and regulatory bodies requires technological accuracy and clear communication about safety protocols, testing processes, and accountability in the event of accidents.

4. E-Commerce and Social Media

Recommender systems targeted ads, and content moderation algorithms shape consumer experiences and public discourse. Trust is critical to avoid perceptions that platforms manipulate users, spread misinformation, or exploit personal data.

Strategies for Building Trust and Credibility

1. Ensure Transparency in AI Processes

Transparency means providing clear information about AI systems work, including their purpose, data usage, and decision-making processes. Companies can:

- Offer plain-language explanations of AI technologies to non-technical audiences.
- Use visual tools like dashboards to show how algorithms function and deliver results.
- Label AI-generated content to avoid confusion or deception (e.g., indicating when recommendations come from automated systems).

2. Establish Ethical Guidelines

Develop and implement ethical principles that guide AI development and deployment. These guidelines should prioritize fairness, inclusivity, diversity, and respect for human rights. Highlight adherence to these principles in communications with stakeholders to foster trust through intentional ethical practices.

3. Engage in Open Communication with Stakeholders

Building trust requires a two-way dialogue between AI developers, businesses, regulators, and end-users. Organizations can achieve this by:

- Hosting forums, town halls, or focus groups where stakeholders can share concerns and feedback.
- Informing users about updates, data collection practices, and system improvements in a clear and timely manner.

4. Adopt Robust Testing and Validation

Regularly test AI systems to ensure accuracy, fairness, and reliability. Continuous testing can reveal flaws, hidden biases, or vulnerabilities, allowing fixes before deployment. Third-party audits also lend credibility by reviewing the system's integrity independently.

5. Implement Human Oversight

AI should supplement human judgment, not replace it. Critical decisions—such as medical diagnoses or financial approvals—should include human oversight to provide a layer of accountability and ethical consideration.

6. Leverage Industry Standards and Regulations

Adhering to established regulations and standards, like the General Data Protection Regulation (GDPR) or AI-specific frameworks, demonstrates a commitment to ethical and lawful practices. These rules help create accountability while setting benchmarks for trust and credibility.

7. Focus on Education and User Empowerment

Empowering users with knowledge about AI works builds familiarity and reduces fear of the unknown. Educational campaigns that cover AI basics, data rights, and safety protocols can help users feel confident and in control when engaging with intelligent systems.

8. Promote Inclusiveness and Fairness

Ensure diverse stakeholders are included during the AI tool design and testing phases. By accounting for various experiences, businesses can minimize biases and create equitable systems for all users.

The Role of Regulations in Fostering Trust

Regulation is an important tool for building public trust in AI technologies. Governments ensure that businesses operate responsibly by setting clear rules for transparency, data privacy, algorithmic accountability, and anti-discrimination practices. Concrete legal frameworks also reassure users that safeguards are in place to protect their interests.

International organizations, governments, and private entities must collaborate to create universal regulations matching AI advancements' pace. This includes establishing industry-specific guidelines, creating ethical review boards, and incentivizing compliance with ethical best practices.

In Conclusion

Building trust and credibility in an AI-driven world is an ongoing endeavor that requires intentionality, collaboration, and a commitment to transparency and fairness. Businesses that prioritize trust will not only foster stronger relationships with their users but also position themselves as leaders in the ethical and responsible use of AI.

By addressing challenges such as transparency, accountability, and ethical concerns, organizations can ensure that AI remains a tool for innovation and empowerment, not a source of fear or inequity. Trust may take time to build, but it is an investment no forward-thinking organization can afford to ignore in a technology-driven future.

Chapter 10
The AI LinkedIn Advantage in Action

Linkedin has long been a staple in professional networking, connecting millions of individuals and businesses across the globe. However, as technology advances, the platform has embraced a new frontier—artificial intelligence (AI). This integration has elevated LinkedIn beyond a digital networking space to a cutting-edge powerhouse for career growth, relationship-building, and business opportunities. With AI at its core, LinkedIn now offers features that make professional interactions more innovative, faster, and more impactful than ever before.

Imagine a networking assistant who intuitively understands your career goals, anticipates your interests, and proposes actionable steps to achieve your aspirations. That's the power AI brings to LinkedIn. Through AI-driven capabilities like personalized job recommendations, dynamic skill assessments, and content curation tailored to your professional interests, LinkedIn has become more than a social network. It has become a personalized career companion, using data and advanced algorithms to create meaningful connections and opportunities tailored to each user.

For example, AI analyzes your profile, career trajectory, and activity on the platform to suggest jobs that align with your skills and aspirations. It enables skill assessments that validate your expertise in key areas, boosting your visibility to recruiters and hiring managers. It curates your feed with industry-specific insights, career advice, and emerging trends, ensuring you stay informed and competitive in your field. AI powers

LinkedIn's messaging tools, helping users break the ice with connection suggestions and tailored conversation starters.

These advancements benefit job seekers as well as entrepreneurs, business leaders, and organizations. Companies can leverage AI to identify top talent, target the right audience for marketing campaigns, and build stronger professional brand identities. Entrepreneurs gain access to smarter networking opportunities, connecting them with potential investors, collaborators, or clients in ways that previously required weeks or even months of effort.

Beyond convenience, these features are reshaping how professionals interact profoundly. They enable more meaningful networking, helping users move beyond surface-level connections to build relationships that drive lasting value. They level the playing field, offering personalized opportunities to all individuals regardless of their location or professional background. And they inject efficiency into professional growth, dramatically reducing the time and effort needed to explore opportunities or showcase expertise.

This chapter uncovers how LinkedIn users and businesses can harness the AI-driven tools that now define the platform. By exploring LinkedIn's evolving features and the underlying technology powering them, we'll reveal how AI is enhancing professional networking and transforming how we approach career development and workplace interactions. From connecting with the right people at the right time to discovering opportunities that align seamlessly with personal and professional goals, LinkedIn's AI revolution empowers users to achieve more in less time.

Welcome to the AI LinkedIn Advantage in Action era—a world where technology meets ambition, propelling careers and businesses forward with precision and purpose. The chapters ahead will unpack these innovations, providing insights into how they work, examples of their impact, and practical tips for leveraging them to their fullest potential. AI is no longer the future for LinkedIn. It's here, reshaping professional networking as we know it. Let's explore how.

The AI LinkedIn Advantage in Action

LinkedIn has long been a staple in professional networking, connecting millions of individuals and businesses across the globe. However, as technology advances, the platform has embraced a new frontier—artificial intelligence (AI). This integration has elevated LinkedIn beyond a digital networking space to a cutting-edge powerhouse for career growth, relationship-building, and business opportunities. With AI at its core, LinkedIn now offers features that make professional interactions more innovative, faster, and more impactful than ever before.

Imagine a networking assistant who intuitively understands your career goals, anticipates your interests, and proposes actionable steps to achieve your aspirations. That's the power AI brings to LinkedIn. Through AI-driven capabilities like personalized job recommendations, dynamic skill assessments, and content curation tailored to your professional interests, LinkedIn has become more than a social network. It has become a personalized career companion, using data and advanced algorithms to create meaningful connections and opportunities tailored to each user.

For example, AI analyzes your profile, career trajectory, and activity on the platform to suggest jobs that align with your skills and aspirations. It enables skill assessments that validate your expertise in key areas, boosting your visibility to recruiters and hiring managers. It curates your feed with industry-specific insights, career advice, and emerging trends, ensuring you stay informed and competitive in your field. AI powers

LinkedIn's messaging tools, helping users break the ice with connection suggestions and tailored conversation starters.

These advancements benefit job seekers as well as entrepreneurs, business leaders, and organizations. Companies can leverage AI to identify top talent, target the right audience for marketing campaigns, and build stronger professional brand identities. Entrepreneurs gain access to smarter networking opportunities, connecting them with potential investors, collaborators, or clients in ways that previously required weeks or even months of effort.

Beyond convenience, these features are reshaping how professionals interact profoundly. They enable more meaningful networking, helping users move beyond surface-level connections to build relationships that drive lasting value. They level the playing field, offering personalized opportunities to all individuals regardless of their location or professional background. And they inject efficiency into professional growth, dramatically reducing the time and effort needed to explore opportunities or showcase expertise.

This chapter uncovers how LinkedIn users and businesses can harness the AI-driven tools that now define the platform. By exploring LinkedIn's evolving features and the underlying technology powering them, we'll reveal how AI is enhancing professional networking and transforming how we approach career development and workplace interactions. From connecting with the right people at the right time to discovering opportunities that align seamlessly with personal and professional goals, LinkedIn's AI revolution empowers users to achieve more in less time.

Welcome to the AI LinkedIn Advantage in Action era—a world where technology meets ambition, propelling careers and businesses forward with precision and purpose. The chapters ahead will unpack these innovations, providing insights into how they work, examples of their impact, and practical tips for leveraging them to their fullest potential. AI is no longer the future for LinkedIn. It's here, reshaping professional networking as we know it. Let's explore how.

Real-Life Success Stories of AI Integration on LinkedIn

Artificial Intelligence (AI) is no longer just a futuristic concept; it's a driving force behind today's most innovative platforms, including LinkedIn. Over the years, LinkedIn has evolved from a simple online professional network to a powerhouse of AI-driven tools and features designed to meet the dynamic needs of modern professionals and businesses. With AI at its core, LinkedIn has empowered users to unlock their full potential by enhancing job searches, networking, branding, and overall success.

This book explores compelling real-life examples of how AI integration on LinkedIn has transformed individuals' careers and propelled businesses' growth. LinkedIn has reshaped how we approach professional interactions, from personalized job recommendations to skill assessments and intelligent content curation. These success stories highlight the far-reaching impact of AI and how it's helping users achieve remarkable outcomes.

Personalized Job Recommendations Leading to Dream Careers

One of AI's most impactful integrations on LinkedIn is its ability to deliver personalized job recommendations. By analyzing a user's profile, work experience, skills, and engagement patterns, LinkedIn's AI tools suggest job opportunities tailored to each individual's career aspirations.

Case Study 1: A Career Shift in Record Time

Maria, a marketing professional with five years of experience, wanted to transition into a data-driven role in digital marketing analytics. She updated her LinkedIn profile to showcase her analytics certifications and recent data-related projects. LinkedIn's AI-powered job recommendation engine suggested several relevant roles in her desired field within days.

Maria applied to a position with a leading tech firm, which had been highlighted among her top recommendations. The employer reached out quickly because her LinkedIn profile was well-optimized and aligned with the role's requirements. Within weeks, Maria landed her dream job with a 30% salary increase and a clear path to growth in her new niche. LinkedIn's AI saved her time and bridged the gap between her skills and the exact opportunities she was seeking.

Case Study 2: Opportunities Without Borders

Mark, an IT professional in Canada, was hesitant to pursue international roles due to the complexity of finding suitable opportunities. However, LinkedIn's AI tools suggested remote and hybrid global company positions based on his keywords and preferences. He applied to a fully remote opportunity with an Australian software firm, impressed the employers during the interview process, and secured a position that required no relocation. Today, Mark proudly works as part of a multinational team, thanks to LinkedIn's AI, which is helping him break geographic barriers.

Skill Assessments Leading to Professional Visibility

Another standout feature of LinkedIn is its skill assessment tool, powered by AI. This feature allows users to take short, objective, skill-specific quizzes to validate their expertise. When users pass these assessments, LinkedIn badges their profile, giving them a competitive edge and increasing visibility to recruiters.

Case Study 3: Turning Certifications into Career Leverage

Sarah, an HR professional, sought to enhance her skillset in digital talent acquisition. To validate her proficiency in these areas, she completed LinkedIn's skill assessments for Applicant Tracking Systems (ATS) and People Analytics. Shortly afterward, she updated her profile to highlight her new badges.

A recruiter who had been searching for professionals with ATS skills came across Sarah's profile and reached out for an interview. Sarah's validated skills stood out, demonstrating that she was well-equipped for the role. Within a month, she was hired by a tech start-up looking for digital-savvy HR leaders.

Case Study 4: Small Wins for Big Opportunities

Jeremy, a freelance graphic designer, wanted to attract more high-paying clients. Using LinkedIn's skill assessments, he earned badges in Adobe Photoshop and User Interface Design. These verified skills improved his profile's ranking in searches by companies looking for freelancers. Within months, Jeremy saw a significant increase in inbound client requests and successfully secured contracts with two major brands.

Intelligent Content Curation Boosts Engagement

AI has also transformed LinkedIn into an invaluable resource for learning and staying informed. By analyzing users' industries, interests, and past engagement, LinkedIn's content curation engine ensures that professionals access the most relevant books, posts, and insights.

Case Study 5: Building Thought Leadership

Emma, the head of digital strategy at a growing media agency, sought to position herself as a thought leader in her field. LinkedIn's AI-curated content feed regularly showed her groundbreaking trends and insights from digital marketing experts. Inspired by these resources, Emma began crafting her LinkedIn posts, adding her unique perspective to ongoing industry discussions.

Her posts gained traction, and within six months, Emma saw her connections grow by 40%. A global media firm noted her thought leadership and invited her to speak at an industry conference. LinkedIn's AI-powered feed not only kept Emma informed but also catalyzed her professional growth.

Case Study 6: Curated Learning for Career Pivots

Anil, a software developer transitioning into product management, leveraged LinkedIn's tailored learning recommendations to prepare for his new career path. He engaged with AI-recommended books, online courses, and career tips specific to product management. Thanks to LinkedIn's curated learning experiences, he had developed a nuanced understanding of the industry by the time he landed his first product management role.

Networking Opportunities Redefined by AI

LinkedIn's core purpose has always been networking, but AI has refined and optimized this process. Users can foster meaningful professional relationships with tools such as "People You May Know," connection insights, and tailored message suggestions.

Case Study 7: From Cold to Warm Connections

Akshay, a business development executive, wanted to connect with hospitality decision-makers. LinkedIn's AI suggested connections based on his region, industry, and mutual connections. Better yet, LinkedIn's messaging assistant helped Akshay craft personalized outreach messages.

Within weeks, Akshay built a network of over 200 contacts in his target industry, converted several leads into business partners, and unlocked contracts worth thousands of dollars. The AI-driven process efficiently minimized cold outreach fails, enabling him to achieve results quickly.

Case Study 8: Strengthening Support for Start-Ups

Sophia, a start-up founder in the sustainability space, used LinkedIn's networking tools to connect with investors and advisors. She secured meetings with five reputable investors by leveraging AI-generated recommendations, including relevant professional groups and events. Two of them later funded her start-up, which is now thriving with an active professional community surrounding its mission.

The Transformative Role of AI in Professional Growth

The success stories above highlight the immense potential of LinkedIn's AI-driven tools in accelerating personal and professional outcomes. Whether landing a dream job, validating key skills, curating learning opportunities, or developing strategic connections, LinkedIn's AI capabilities empower professionals to achieve more than they could through manual efforts alone.

More than a feature, AI on LinkedIn is truly a game-changer. It personalizes the user experience, making job markets more accessible, bridging networks across the globe, and enhancing professional growth like never before. By integrating cutting-edge technology with human potential, LinkedIn is shaping a future where success is within reach for every individual and business ready to harness these tools.

Step-by-Step Implementation of Your AI-Driven Strategy

Harnessing the power of Artificial Intelligence (AI) is no longer a luxury for businesses—it's a necessity in a competitive, data-driven world. By adopting an AI-driven strategy, organizations can unlock greater efficiencies, deliver enhanced customer experiences, and gain a crucial edge. However, implementing AI effectively requires careful planning and execution. Done right, it empowers businesses to innovate, improve decision-making, reduce costs, and scale operations.

This book outlines a clear step-by-step approach for businesses developing and implementing a robust AI-driven strategy. From identifying needs to ensuring seamless adoption, we will walk through the key stages of creating a future-proof AI strategy.

1. Assess Business Needs and Define Clear Objectives

The foundation of a successful AI strategy starts with introspection—understanding why your organization needs AI and what you hope to achieve. Rushing into AI adoption without clear goals can waste time, resources, and frustration.

- **Identify Pain Points:** Start by analyzing business challenges and inefficiencies. For example, are you struggling to predict customer demand, automate repetitive tasks, or personalize marketing efforts?
- **Set SMART Goals:** Define Specific, Measurable, Achievable, Relevant, and Time-bound objectives. For example, a goal might be to reduce customer churn by 20% using predictive analytics within 12 months.

- **Understand Opportunities:** Recognize areas where AI can create new value, such as optimizing costs, entering new markets, or improving customer satisfaction.

Example:

A retail business may use AI to optimize inventory management by leveraging predictive analytics to minimize overstock and stockouts, saving costs and improving efficiency.

2. Identify the Right AI Technologies and Tools

AI is not a one-size-fits-all solution. Different industries and business functions require varying types of AI technologies. Research and choose tools that align with your specific objectives.

- **Understand AI Types:** Identify what type of AI aligns with your goals. Examples include machine learning for predictions, natural language processing (NLP) for customer interactions, or image recognition for quality control.
- **Evaluate Solutions:** Compare off-the-shelf AI solutions versus building in-house expertise. Prebuilt platforms are often faster to implement, while tailored solutions can better address unique requirements.
- **Select Vendors:** Investigate technology providers and platforms. Look for vendors with proven expertise, solid customer reviews, and transparent data security practices.

Example:

A healthcare organization aiming to improve patient diagnostics might adopt AI tools that analyze medical imaging, such as X-rays, leveraging machine learning to identify abnormalities.

3. Prepare and Manage Your Data

AI's effectiveness hinges on the quality of the data it processes. Clean, well-organized, and secure data ensures accurate predictions, insights, and outcomes.

- **Assess Data Availability:** Review the data your organization already collects and identify gaps. Does your team gather enough data in the right formats to power AI systems?
- **Ensure Data Quality:** Poor-quality data leads to poor results. Invest in cleaning and standardizing data to eliminate errors and inconsistencies.
- **Focus on Security and Privacy:** Protect sensitive data using encryption, firewalls, and access controls. Review compliance requirements such as GDPR or HIPAA to ensure ethical and lawful data handling.
- **Leverage Data Platforms:** Use centralized platforms or data lakes to efficiently store, organize, and retrieve large datasets for analysis.

Example:

A transportation company might collect detailed location and traffic data across fleets to train algorithms that optimize delivery routes, resulting in faster service and lower fuel costs.

4. Integrate AI Tools into Existing Systems

For AI to drive impact, it must seamlessly integrate with your organization's systems and workflows. Plan for smooth integration to avoid disruptions.

- **Conduct Pilot Tests:** Before company-wide implementation, roll out AI tools on a smaller scale. For example, target a single department or process. Use pilot tests to gather feedback and address integration challenges early.

- **Adopt APIs and Middleware:** Application programming interfaces (APIs) connect new AI tools with existing databases, platforms, or software.
- **Ensure Scalability:** Choose AI tools that can scale as your organization grows or require additional features and capabilities.
- **Monitor Compatibility:** Confirm that employees can easily access new solutions without requiring complete infrastructure overhauls.

Example:

A financial services firm adopting a chatbot for customer support might integrate it with its existing CRM (Customer Relationship Management) system to allow seamless retrieval of customer records.

5. Train Your Workforce and Foster Change Management

AI implementation isn't just a technical challenge—it's a people challenge. For AI tools to succeed, employees must understand, trust, and adopt them.

- **Provide Training:** Conduct hands-on training workshops or online courses tailored to different user levels. Ensure employees know when and how to use AI tools effectively.
- **Address Resistance:** Employees may fear that AI threatens their jobs. Engage in transparent communication to address concerns and highlight how AI will augment, not replace their work.
- **Create AI Ambassadors:** Identify tech-savvy or enthusiastic employees to champion AI adoption in their teams and provide peer support.

- **Foster a Culture of Innovation:** Encourage collaboration, experimentation, and openness to change within your organization.

Example:

An educational institution adopting AI-driven grading systems can train teachers to interpret outputs correctly and emphasize how automation frees their time for mentorship and personalized support.

6. Monitor, Adjust, and Scale Implementation

AI isn't a one-and-done solution. Once systems are in place, ongoing monitoring, refinement, and scaling are crucial to long-term success.

- **Monitor Performance Metrics:** Track KPIs (Key Performance Indicators) such as accuracy rates, cost savings, or user satisfaction. This helps identify whether AI tools are achieving their intended goals.
- **Optimize Algorithms:** Regularly update and retrain AI tools with fresh data to improve results and address changing business needs or market conditions.
- **Gather Feedback:** Gather insights from employees and customers to spot areas for improvement or additional features. Feedback loops help refine AI tools.
- **Develop a Scaling Plan:** Scale successful pilots across more teams, departments, or regions. Ensure sufficient infrastructure and talent resources to support wider use.

Example:

A logistics firm monitoring its AI-powered route optimization found that implementing the tool globally saved 15% in fuel costs. Based on these results, the firm expanded its use to all regions.

7. Learn from Industry Success Stories

Finally, draw inspiration and practical knowledge from organizations that successfully implement AI-driven strategies in their fields.

Case Studies:

- **Manufacturing Industry:** A manufacturing company uses AI to reduce waste in its supply chain by analyzing production data. Within two years, this saved millions of dollars and improved sustainability.
- **Retail Sector:** A global e-commerce brand integrated AI chatbots for faster customer support, reducing response times by 60% while increasing satisfaction scores.
- **Healthcare:** An AI-powered diagnostic tool helped a hospital system reduce diagnostic errors in radiology, leading to better patient outcomes and fewer legal challenges.

The Bottom Line

Implementing an AI-driven strategy is a transformative endeavor, but it requires careful planning and execution. Each step lays the foundation for success, from setting clear objectives to integrating tools, managing data, training employees, and scaling solutions. The benefits, however, are undeniable—businesses that adopt AI effectively open doors to unprecedented efficiency, insights, and growth.

With a clear and deliberate approach, your organization can harness AI's power to survive and thrive in an increasingly competitive, tech-driven world. Start strategizing today to stay steps ahead of the curve!

Overcoming Challenges While Using AI on LinkedIn

Artificial Intelligence (AI) has transformed LinkedIn into a sophisticated platform for professional growth, networking, and career advancement. With features like personalized job recommendations, skill assessments, and content curation, AI-powered tools offer users unparalleled opportunities to enhance their professional journeys. However, alongside these benefits, challenges such as data privacy concerns, algorithmic biases, and the complexity of AI features can complicate the experience.

To fully harness the potential of AI on LinkedIn, users and businesses must address these challenges head-on. This book explores the most common obstacles, their implications, and actionable strategies to overcome them. Additionally, we'll share examples of how users and companies have successfully navigated these complexities to make the platform work for them.

Understanding Common Challenges

Before exploring solutions, let's discuss the top challenges LinkedIn users face when engaging with AI-driven tools.

1. Data Privacy Concerns

AI relies heavily on user data to deliver personalized features. While this enables smarter recommendations and curated content, it raises concerns about how data is collected, stored, and used. Users may worry about privacy, particularly when sensitive personal or professional information is involved.

For example:

- Professionals might hesitate to update their profiles with significant career changes, fearing unintended exposure or misuse of their information.
- Businesses using LinkedIn for recruitment face scrutiny in ensuring their candidates' data remains secure.

Impact: Without confidence in LinkedIn's data protection practices, users may limit how much they engage with the platform's AI features, missing out on valuable opportunities.

2. Algorithmic Biases

AI algorithms are only as unbiased as the data they are trained on. LinkedIn's AI tools may inadvertently favor certain demographics, job titles, or regions based on historical data patterns. This can lead to unintended outcomes, such as:

- Job recommendations that fail to consider diverse career paths or skill sets.
- Content curation that reinforces limited industry-specific perspectives rather than broadening horizons.
- Such biases can disadvantage certain individuals or groups, undermining equity and inclusivity on the platform.

Impact: Algorithmic biases damage trust, creating frustration for users who feel unfairly overlooked by AI systems.

3. Complexity of AI Features

While LinkedIn's AI tools are powerful, their complexity may overwhelm users who are unfamiliar with them. Features like skill assessments, advanced filters, or tailored insights require effort to understand and use effectively.

For example:

- Users may struggle to interpret job matches if they know how LinkedIn calculates relevance.
- A small business might face difficulty leveraging AI analytics for hiring without proper guidance.

Impact: If tools are seen as too complex, users may hesitate to adopt them, diminishing their overall LinkedIn experience.

4. Transparency Issues

AI systems often operate as "black boxes," making decisions or recommendations that are unclear to the user. For instance:

- Why has a particular job been recommended to someone?
- On what basis is content pushed forward in the news feed?

This lack of transparency can frustrate users and stifle their confidence in the AI's reliability.

Impact: A lack of transparency can lead to skepticism and disengagement, reducing trust in LinkedIn's AI services.

Strategies to Overcome Challenges

Now that we've outlined the barriers let's uncover strategies and solutions to ensure LinkedIn's AI tools work effectively for everyone.

1. Strengthening Data Privacy

To address privacy concerns, LinkedIn users and businesses must adopt practices that enhance security while enabling AI's functionality.

What LinkedIn Can Do:

- **Transparent Data Policies:** Provide users with clear information about the data collected and its use. Transparency builds trust.
- **Advanced Privacy Controls:** Users can customize data-sharing settings, choosing how much personal information they are comfortable sharing for AI analysis.

What Users Can Do:

- **Review Privacy Settings:** Regularly update privacy controls to ensure only necessary data is visible on the platform.
- **Monitor Profile Updates:** Be mindful of any sensitive information shared online.

Example: Joanna's graphic designer updated her privacy settings after learning how LinkedIn's AI uses profile data. This allowed her to safely enhance her profile while limiting unnecessary exposure to third parties.

2. Tackling Algorithmic Biases

Reducing biases in AI systems requires conscious collaboration between LinkedIn, businesses, and its users.

What LinkedIn Can Do:

- **Diversify Data Inputs:** Train algorithms with diverse datasets that reflect various career fields, demographics, and experiences.
- **Audit AI Models Regularly:** Regularly test and fine-tune algorithms to identify and correct potential biases.

What Users Can Do:

- **Voice Feedback:** Report instances where recommendations or content seem biased. Feedback helps platforms refine their AI systems.
- **Engage Proactively:** Add various skills, experiences, and keywords to profiles to better influence AI outputs.

Example: A mid-level project manager reported skewed job recommendations only for entry-level positions. LinkedIn's support team worked to refine its system, and within weeks, the recommendations improved.

3. Simplifying AI Features

To make AI tools feel more approachable, users and businesses need access to supportive resources and practical use cases.

What LinkedIn Can Do:

- **User Tutorials:** Offer clear, step-by-step guides or videos on using advanced features such as skill assessments or tailored job searches.
- **Onboarding Tools:** Walk new users or business accounts through AI features in their early registration phase.

What Users Can Do:

- **Invest Time in Learning:** Explore LinkedIn Learning courses specifically focused on optimizing AI-driven tools for networking or recruitment.
- **Start Small:** Begin using one AI feature (e.g., job recommendations) before exploring others.

Example: Sarah, a small business recruiter, initially felt overwhelmed by LinkedIn's AI analytics. After completing a tutorial and engaging with LinkedIn's customer support, she successfully utilized its recruitment algorithms to hire three qualified candidates.

4. Promoting AI Transparency

Greater clarity is needed for users to trust the decisions and suggestions being made by AI systems.

What LinkedIn Can Do:

- **Explain Recommendations:** Add explanations to AI-driven features, such as why a particular piece of content appeared in a feed or why a job was recommended.

- **Provide Insights Settings:** Offer a behind-the-scenes view for users to adjust what factors are prioritized in AI recommendations (e.g., location, experience).

What Users Can Do:

- **Experiment with Inputs:** Modify profile information and observe changes in recommendations. Understanding these patterns can help users better customize their experience.

Example: Anil used LinkedIn's "Why was this shown to me?" feature attached to job recommendations. The AI adapted and filtered more relevant roles aligned with his career aspirations by tweaking his job preferences.

Success Stories of Overcoming Challenges

Here are examples of users and businesses that persevered, overcoming AI-related challenges to achieve significant results:

1. **A Marketing Professional's Transparency Win:** A marketing strategist leveraged LinkedIn's AI-powered job search but initially felt the algorithm wasn't aligned with her goals. She refined her profile content and explored the platform's feedback mechanisms. Within a few weeks, she landed a position tailored to her skills and interests.

2. **Business Scaling with Simplified AI:** A start-up in sustainable energy initially struggled to understand LinkedIn's audience-targeting insights. After training staff and adopting AI-powered tools step-by-step, they experienced a 25% increase in quality leads.

3. **Reducing Inefficiency Through User Support:** A hiring firm raised concerns about irrelevant matches during LinkedIn's

early AI iterations. They reduced recruitment timelines by half by collaborating with LinkedIn's team to refine the algorithm.

In Conclusion

Overcoming challenges while using AI on LinkedIn requires a proactive approach by LinkedIn itself, professionals, and businesses. By enhancing data privacy, addressing biases, simplifying features, and promoting transparency, users can leverage AI to drive meaningful outcomes. AI tools offer incredible career and business development opportunities, and with thoughtful strategies, these challenges can be transformed into gateways for success.

When users and platforms collaborate to address these obstacles, a more inclusive, efficient, and effective professional networking space results. With the right mindset and resources, LinkedIn's AI is a tool that empowers everyone to thrive in a digitally connected world.

Creating a Long-Term AI-enhanced LinkedIn Plan

LinkedIn is more than a digital resume—it's a dynamic platform where professionals and businesses can build networks, grow careers, and cultivate thought leadership. Artificial Intelligence (AI) integration has taken LinkedIn's capabilities to new heights, making it a powerful tool for personalized networking, content optimization, and data-driven decision-making. However, to truly unlock its potential, one needs a long-term AI-enhanced LinkedIn plan.

By strategically leveraging AI, professionals and businesses can increase engagement and visibility and stay ahead in their careers and industries. This book provides a step-by-step guide to developing a sustainable, AI-driven LinkedIn strategy for long-term success, with actionable insights, tools, and real-life examples.

Why AI-Enhancement Matters for LinkedIn

LinkedIn's AI-driven features go far beyond recommendations and connections. From intelligent content curation to advanced analytics, the platform provides tools that empower users to tailor their professional presence. A long-term AI-enhanced plan ensures sustained growth by doing the following:

- **Personalizing Experiences:** AI allows networking and job-hunting strategies to adapt to individual goals and preferences.
- **Improving Visibility:** By understanding how the platform's algorithms work, you can optimize content to reach a wider audience.
- **Streamlining Processes:** AI automates time-consuming tasks like outreach, profile optimization, and content recommendations.
- **Driving Smart Decisions:** AI-powered analytics provide actionable insights to refine your strategies.

With these advantages, adopting a long-term LinkedIn plan is essential for staying relevant in a fast-paced professional landscape.

Steps to Develop a Long-Term AI-Enhanced LinkedIn Plan

1. Define Your Objectives

The first step in creating you plan to establish clear and measurable goals. What do you want to achieve on LinkedIn? Your objectives will shape every aspect of your AI strategy.

- **Identify Personal or Business Goals:** Are you looking to land a new job, build a personal brand, or establish your company as a thought leader?

- **Set SMART Goals:** Your goals should be Specific, Measurable, Achievable, Relevant, and Time-bound. For example, "Increase profile views by 30% in six months by publishing regular LinkedIn books" is a solid SMART goal.
- **Balance Short-Term and Long-Term Vision:** Short-term wins, such as increasing followers, should align with broader ambitions, like becoming a trusted voice in your field.

2. Leverage AI Tools for Personalized Networking

Personalized networking is one of LinkedIn's strongest suits, and AI drives it with unparalleled efficiency. Use LinkedIn's features to build meaningful connections that align with your goals.

- **AI Recommendations:** Explore the "People You May Know" and "Suggested Profiles" feature to identify potential connections.
- **Intelligent Messaging Tools:** Use AI-generated suggestions to reach out. For example, personalize messages using LinkedIn's templates to demonstrate shared values or interests when connecting with someone.
- **Endorsements and Skill Validation:** Leverage AI to identify and validate skills within your network, boosting your credibility and that of your connections.

Example:

A mid-level manager used AI-curated "Who Viewed Your Profile" insights to contact recruiters actively searching for candidates in her field. She connected with them through personalized messages and ultimately secured valuable interviews.

3. Optimize Content for AI Algorithms

Your content is key to establishing your professional reputation on LinkedIn. By understanding and leveraging AI algorithms, you can enhance the visibility of your posts and updates.

- **Consistency Matters:** Regular posting signals to the algorithm that you are an active and valuable contributor. Aim to post at least two to three times a week.
- **Use Relevant Hashtags:** AI prioritizes tailored content. Choose hashtags that align with your industry and personal brand (e.g., #DataAnalytics, #LeadershipTips).
- **Engage with Your Network:** The AI system rewards posts that generate dialogue. Respond to comments, ask questions, and actively engage with others' updates.
- **AI-Driven Content Suggestions:** Use tools like LinkedIn's Trending Insights to stay updated on what topics are gaining traction within your industry.

Example:

A young entrepreneur gained thousands of followers by posting short video updates with AI-detected trending hashtags like #StartUpLife and engaging her audience in the comments. This boosted her visibility and expanded her reach globally.

4. Use AI Analytics to Track Progress

Without tracking your progress, you cannot know if your LinkedIn strategy is working. AI-powered analytics provide deep insights into what's resonating with your audience.

- **Track Key Metrics:** Focus on parameters like post impressions, engagement rate, connection growth, and profile views. Use these metrics to evaluate the effectiveness of your strategy.
- **Leverage LinkedIn Content Suggestions:** Review LinkedIn's analytics to see which posts perform well and why. Invest in creating similar content to generate consistent engagement.
- **Monitor Job Application Metrics:** When applying for positions, AI tools will show statistics about recruiters viewing your profile. Use this data to refine your applications.

Example:

A digital marketer closely monitored engagement rates on her posts and noticed that posts with infographics performed better than written updates. She developed visually appealing content using these insights, leading to a 40% increase in overall engagement.

5. Continuous Learning and Adaptation

AI is constantly evolving, as is how professionals and businesses interact on LinkedIn. To sustain long-term growth, you must remain agile and willing to learn.

- **Stay Updated on AI Trends:** Follow LinkedIn Learning courses or thought leaders in AI and professional development to stay ahead of new tools and strategies.
- **Adapt to Platform Changes:** LinkedIn frequently updates its algorithms and features. Review release notes regularly to understand how these changes can impact your strategy.
- **Test, Evaluate, Repeat:** Treat your LinkedIn plan as a series of experiments. That's how you'll discover what works best—and what doesn't.

Example:

A small-business owner used LinkedIn Learning to upskill in AI-driven marketing strategies. By revising her content approach based on new techniques, she doubled her follower count within a year.

6. Build a Trusted Digital Brand

Long-term success on LinkedIn requires more than occasional engagement. You must craft a digital identity that others trust and want to follow.

- **Establish Consistency:** Maintain a consistent voice and visual style in your posts. For example, use the same profile picture, banner, and tone.
- **Showcase Thought Leadership:** Share insights drawn from your experience. Back up your claims with data and examples to demonstrate authority.
- **Encourage Recommendations:** Ask colleagues or clients for LinkedIn endorsements and testimonials highlighting your expertise.

Example:

A freelance writer used her AI-powered content analytics to consistently identify topics her audience found valuable, establishing herself as a reliable source for advice on freelancing. Over time, this niche focus brought her numerous contracts through LinkedIn.

Benefits of a Long-Term AI Strategy

When properly implemented, a long-term AI-enhanced LinkedIn plan provides significant benefits:

- **Enhanced Visibility:** By aligning with AI recommendations, your posts and profile achieve greater reach.

- **Streamlined Automation:** From job hunting to networking, AI simplifies processes, saving time and effort.
- **Deeper Insights:** Advanced analytics allow you to make data-driven decisions for sustained growth.
- **Global Connections:** AI tools break down geographic barriers, enabling seamless networking with professionals worldwide.
- **Adaptability:** Continuous learning ensures you stay relevant in an evolving platform.

In Conclusion

Creating a long-term AI-enhanced LinkedIn plan is an investment in your professional growth and networking potential. You can unlock new opportunities and achieve sustained success by defining clear objectives, leveraging AI for personalized networking, optimizing content for algorithms, and using analytics to refine strategies.

The key lies in being proactive and flexible. LinkedIn's AI evolves rapidly, and by staying informed and adaptable, you can remain a step ahead, ensuring your plan keeps delivering value over time. Whether you're an individual professional or a business, the roadmap to long-term LinkedIn success is now in your hands. Start building your AI-enhanced strategy today and watch your network—and opportunities—flourish.

Final Thoughts

Artificial Intelligence (AI) is no longer just a futuristic concept; it has become a pivotal driver of change, redefining professional networking and engagement on platforms like LinkedIn. Throughout this book, we have explored the profound ways AI enhances the professional landscape. Automating mundane tasks, offering personalized solutions, and delivering data-driven insights have empowered professionals to network more efficiently and intelligently. Whether it's optimizing profiles for maximum visibility, tailoring job searches, or identifying meaningful connections, AI has transformed what was once a passive online experience into an active, strategic tool for growth.

One of the most significant advantages of AI lies in its ability to personalize experiences. LinkedIn's algorithms analyze user behaviors, preferences, and activities to provide customized recommendations, ensuring every job posting, network suggestion, or content piece is relevant and impactful. This personalization makes networking more manageable and meaningful, as AI helps bridge gaps between shared interests, mutual goals, and professional synergies. However, this convenience requires users to be proactive in curating their digital presence and staying informed about how AI drives these interactions.

At the heart of these advancements lies actionable insight. AI-powered analytics enable professionals to learn from their engagement metrics, clarifying what works and what doesn't. Whether crafting compelling content, identifying trends, or tracking professional growth, these insights help optimize strategies, adding a layer of precision to decision-making that wasn't possible before. This capability is a game-changer for businesses—it facilitates targeted campaigns, strategic recruiting, and stronger relationships with audiences. AI has essentially rewritten the rules of engagement, creating opportunities for deeper connections and sustained impact.

However, any discussion about AI's potential would be incomplete without acknowledging its challenges. Ethical AI usage remains a critical concern. From data privacy to algorithmic biases, ensuring transparency and fairness is essential within this rapidly evolving space. Businesses and individuals must prioritize ethical considerations, respect user data, and leverage AI in ways that foster trust, inclusion, and accountability. This isn't simply about preventing misuse—it's about building trust in a world where digital and professional boundaries are increasingly intertwined.

Success in leveraging AI also demands a mindset of adaptability and continuous learning. AI is not static; it evolves rapidly, introducing new tools and capabilities that professionals must understand to remain competitive. Staying ahead means investing in upskilling, following emerging trends, and revisiting strategies to align with new opportunities that AI offers. Professionals who remain curious and open to experimenting with AI-driven solutions will secure their relevance in an environment that rewards innovation and flexibility.

Looking ahead, the future of AI in LinkedIn and professional networking promises endless possibilities, but it also comes with new responsibilities. AI tools will continue to become more innovative and intuitive, creating new levels of engagement while breaking down geographical and industry barriers. However, these advancements will require users to balance automation and authenticity. There will be an even greater need for professionals to maintain genuine connections and personalized interactions amidst AI's efficiency.

For businesses, the challenge will be integrating AI in ways that align with organizational goals while fostering a human-centered approach. The most successful strategies will combine AI's ability to scale operations and analyze data with human efforts' emotional intelligence and creativity. These complementary elements will define the next era of professional networking, enabling businesses and individuals to form stronger, more impactful relationships.

It is vital for professionals and organizations to act now to tap into this potential. AI tools should not just supplement traditional strategies—they should become integral to how you approach your career, connect with others, and achieve your goals. Begin by exploring available AI tools, experimenting with features like advanced analytics, and familiarizing yourself with LinkedIn's recommendation systems. Take small but consistent steps to integrate AI, evaluate its impact, and refine your approach as you learn.

The transformations brought about by AI on LinkedIn are only the beginning of a broader shift that will redefine how we work, connect, and innovate. Those who actively engage with these changes will gain a competitive advantage and position themselves as thought leaders in their fields. By fully understanding AI's possibilities and limitations, you can shape your professional future and contribute to a more connected, efficient, and inclusive professional world.

Now is your time to act. Incorporate the insights in this book into your professional strategy, remain flexible in your approach, and lean into the opportunities that AI presents. With thoughtful implementation and an open mindset, you can unlock your full potential and thrive in the AI-driven professional landscape. The future belongs to those who adapt to change and lead it. Harness the power of AI, and propel yourself and your organization into a future brimming with innovation and success.

WHAT IS THE NEXT STEP

Congratulations on your achievement in completing *The AI LinkedIn Advantage: Unleash the Power of AI and Dominate the Competition*! This book has not only inspired you, but also equipped you with the tools and strategies to stand out, connect, and ultimately dominate your competition on LinkedIn. You should be proud of your progress and motivated to apply these learnings.

With the power of AI, you now have the means to master your personal brand. This book has shown you how to craft a LinkedIn profile that not only gets noticed, but also builds trust, credibility, and authority in your field. Your profile is now more than a digital resume—it's your gateway to limitless opportunities, all made possible with the help of AI.

When it comes to networking, the strategies in this book enable you to approach it with precision and purpose. AI tools make it easier than ever to connect with the right people, whether they be collaborators, customers, or key decision-makers. This isn't just networking—it's strategic networking that drives results by connecting you with the people who matter most to your professional success.

Your content strategy has likely undergone a significant transformation. With guidance on creating posts and updates that captivate and connect, you're now positioned to cut through the noise and engage your audience like never before. You've seen how AI can help you present your ideas in a way that resonates and inspires action. This transformation should leave you feeling empowered and confident in your content strategy.

But this book isn't just about concepts; it's about execution. You've explored actionable insights supported by real-world examples, ensuring you can apply the techniques with confidence, no matter your experience level. From beginners to seasoned professionals, the step-by-step guidance ensures there's value for everyone. This should leave you feeling secure and knowledgeable about the concepts you've learned.

And throughout this journey, you've had access to tried-and-tested advice from my professional experience. My goal has been to share insider tips that empower you to make LinkedIn your competitive advantage. The lessons in these chapters are designed to set you apart and give you the tools to dominate your industry.

Now, it's time to take action. Whether revamping your profile, planning your next post, or connecting with the right person, remember this book is your guide. As you grow, keep returning to these pages for ideas, strategy adjustments, and fresh inspiration.

LinkedIn is your stage, AI is your edge, and now you hold the playbook. Go forward, implement these lessons, and start realizing your full potential. And, of course, don't hesitate to reach out with your questions or share your successes. You can find me on LinkedIn or email me directly at Akushner@LinkedVantage.com. I can't wait to see the fantastic results you'll achieve!

Here's to your LinkedIn success—your future starts now

Bonus
Download

SCAN ME

WORKING WITH AL KUSHNER

Al Kushner is one of the most sought-after LinkedIn and social-selling keynote speakers, trainers, and consultants in the industry today. Known for his expertise and dynamic approach, Al collaborates with companies across the globe, traveling to diverse destinations and seamlessly supporting events and businesses virtually wherever they may be.

Suppose you're looking to unlock the full potential of LinkedIn and social selling for your company, team, or business. In that case, Al Kushner is the expert to whom to turn. His tailored strategies and actionable insights deliver accurate results, empowering professionals to thrive in today's competitive landscape.

Due to his high demand, Al is often booked months in advance. However, he is available for various engagements, including keynote speeches, customized training sessions, corporate workshops, and virtual consultations. Don't miss the chance to work with one of the most impactful voices in LinkedIn and social selling—get in touch to secure your spot today!

- **Corporate LinkedIn, Social Selling & Sales Navigator Training**
  Offer tailored training programs to help organizations master LinkedIn tools, social selling techniques, and Sales Navigator for measurable growth and enhanced sales performance.

- **Advanced LinkedIn Growth Consulting**
  Provide expert consultancy to accelerate LinkedIn growth strategies, optimize company profiles, and maximize business lead generation opportunities.

- **Investor & Advisor Services**

  Collaborate with businesses and startups as investors and advisors, offering insights and strategic guidance to achieve sustainable growth and success.

- **Executive Personal Branding Coaching**

  I will work one-on-one with executives to build compelling LinkedIn profiles, strengthen their personal brands, and establish authority in their industries.

You can find out more right here – LinkedVantage.com

INTERNATIONAL KEYNOTE SPEAKER

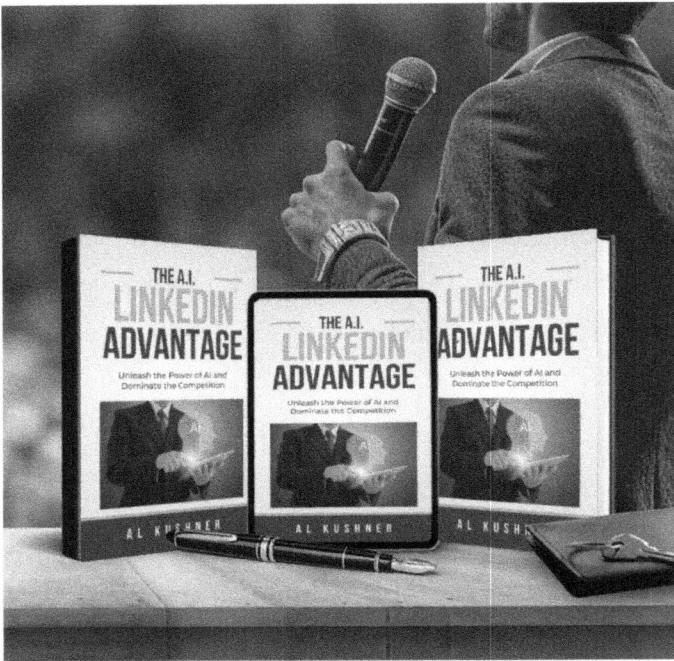

'Al captivated the audience with an electrifying keynote presentation, brimming with passion and expertise, unveiling the game-changing power of LinkedIn and AI.'

Whether in person worldwide or virtually from his state-of-the-art studio with top-tier camera, lighting, and audio, Al delivers dynamic, impactful presentations you won't forget. Book now for an unforgettable experience!

BRAND-NEW KEYNOTE WITH THIS BOOK

"Mastering LinkedIn Networking with the Power of AI"

Discover how AI revolutionizes LinkedIn networking by identifying high-value connections, crafting smarter engagement strategies, and automating follow-ups to build meaningful relationships faster.

Why not elevate your next event by having Al Kushner take the stage and captivate your audience with his dynamic keynote presentations? And here's the perfect added bonus—gift your team, company, or event attendees a copy of his groundbreaking book or audiobook, *The AI LinkedIn Advantage*. Special pricing is available for delegates when you include books, with discounts tailored to audience size.

This is a unique opportunity to combine inspiring ideas with actionable insights while leaving attendees with a tangible resource to maximize their success. To inquire about booking Al for your next SKO, conference, or event, simply email your dates and details to Akushner@LinkedVantage.com. Don't wait—secure a truly unforgettable experience today!

Bonus
Download

SCAN ME

Empower Your Group with a Customized LinkedIn Presentation

Are you looking to inspire and empower your group or organization with actionable insights that drive success? I'd be thrilled to share my expertise and passion for LinkedIn. This platform can transform how we grow, connect, and achieve professional goals.

With an in-depth understanding of LinkedIn's strategies, tools, and best practices, I immediately bring real-world knowledge that your audience can use. My talks are more than presentations—they're opportunities to unlock new possibilities for career advancement, strategic networking, and personal branding.

What Sets His Presentations Apart?

- **Customized Content**: Each presentation is tailored to your group's unique needs and goals. Whether your organization is focused on landing job opportunities, building stronger networks, or amplifying brand visibility, you'll receive a session that hits the mark.
- **Engaging Delivery**: My lively and approachable speaking style ensures your audience stays engaged, energized, and motivated to take action.
- **Practical Takeaways**: Your group will leave with clear, actionable steps and a renewed sense of purpose to make LinkedIn work for them, feeling equipped and ready to implement the strategies.

Formats to Suit Your Needs

He offers in-person and virtual options, ensuring flexibility that aligns with your organization's schedule and preferences. Every session is designed to equip your team with the tools and inspiration to elevate their LinkedIn presence and achieve professional success, making your audience feel accommodated and considered.

Topics include

1. **Maximizing LinkedIn for Small Business Success**

   Strategies for building brand visibility, generating leads, and connecting with potential clients on LinkedIn.

2. **LinkedIn for Solopreneurs and Entrepreneurs**

   How to leverage LinkedIn to grow your business, establish authority, and expand your professional network.

3. **Recruitment Strategies on LinkedIn for Companies**

   Best practices for finding, attracting, and retaining top talent through LinkedIn's recruitment tools and posts.

4. **Crafting a Job Seeker's Personal Brand on LinkedIn**

   Tips for creating an attention-grabbing profile, connecting with recruiters, and standing out in the job market.

5. **LinkedIn for Non-Profits**

   Building relationships with donors, recruiting volunteers, and finding passionate Board members on LinkedIn.

6. **LinkedIn for Social Media Skeptics**

   Overcoming the fear of online networking and finding authentic ways to engage on LinkedIn without feeling overwhelmed.

7. **Personal Branding Made Simple on LinkedIn**

   How professionals can tell their stories and showcase their expertise to build a unique and memorable profile.

8. **Boosting Engagement with LinkedIn Content**

   Understanding what to share and how to craft posts that drive conversations and increase visibility.

9. **LinkedIn Networking Secrets for Entrepreneurial Growth**

   Using targeted strategies on LinkedIn, practical ways to connect with mentors, investors, or collaborators.

10. **The Power of LinkedIn Groups for Professional Growth**

   Exploring how to find and engage with niche communities that add value to your career or business objectives.

LINKEDIN, SOCIAL SELLING &
SALES NAVIGATOR TRAINING

"Investing in Al Kushner's social selling program delivered tangible results, adding $1–$2 USD million to our bottom line."

Al Kushner is recognized as one of the world's most renowned LinkedIn and social selling trainers. With an unparalleled passion for empowering professionals, Al provides a comprehensive range of training solutions tailored to meet the diverse needs of individuals, teams, and organizations.

His training options are designed to deliver impactful results, whether you want to master the basics or elevate your current LinkedIn strategy. Participants can choose from dynamic and immersive experiences, including:

- **1-Day and 2-Day LinkedIn Masterclasses**
  Intense in-person sessions packed with actionable strategies to supercharge your LinkedIn presence.

- **12-Week LinkedIn Social Selling Corporate Training Programs**

  Comprehensive corporate programs that transform teams into social selling powerhouses.

- **Sales Navigator Mastery Training**

  A specialized course for leveraging Sales Navigator to its full potential and driving measurable outcomes.

- **Social Selling Mastery Training**

  Advanced social selling techniques to generate leads, build relationships, and close deals effectively.

- **LinkedIn Boot Camps**

  Fast-paced, targeted sessions to kick-start LinkedIn success with hands-on guidance.

- **Custom Training Packages**

  Flexible and personalized solutions for organizations with unique goals and challenges.

Al's expertise and engaging approach equip participants with the skills, techniques, and confidence they need to dominate on LinkedIn and beyond. Whether your focus is personal branding, lead generation, or team-wide transformation, Al Kushner is the trainer you need to partner with. Elevate your LinkedIn game today and unlock unparalleled success.

The AI LinkedIn Advantage Content Masterclass

Take your team's LinkedIn content game to new heights with Al Kushner's **2.5-hour LinkedIn Content Masterclass**, inspired by his groundbreaking book, *The AI LinkedIn Advantage: Unleash the Power of AI and Dominate the Competition*! This dynamic and interactive session is tailored to help your team or company master **all forms of LinkedIn content creation** by leveraging the power of AI tools.

What to Expect:

- **AI-Driven Content Strategies**

  Learn how to use cutting-edge AI techniques to craft compelling LinkedIn posts that break through the noise and resonate with your audience.

- **Interactive Live Content Creation**

  This session is not just about theory—it goes hands-on. Your team will be guided to create, refine, and publish LinkedIn content live during the training, fostering real-time collaboration and immediate results.

- **Practical Training Designed for Impact**

  The masterclass focuses on actionable ideas and proven methods to help attendees enhance their personal brands, build strong connections, and create a lasting impact on LinkedIn.

Training Packages Include:

- **Physical or Digital Copies of the Book**

  Every participant will receive a copy of *The AI LinkedIn Advantage*, ensuring the concepts covered in the session become a lasting resource.

- **Ongoing Online LinkedIn Training**
  Additional online tools and resources are provided post-session to keep your team learning and growing.

Flexible Delivery Options:

- **Global Availability**
  Al Kushner is available to deliver this training anywhere in the world, in person.

- **Virtual Training from a State-of-the-Art Studio**
  Engage in an immersive virtual experience with Al's high-spec camera, lighting, and microphone setup, ensuring crystal-clear quality and an engaging session for all participants.

Transform your team into a LinkedIn content powerhouse with this one-of-a-kind masterclass based on Al's award-winning expertise. To inquire about booking this session for your team or company, email your dates and details to **Akushner@LinkedVantage.com**.

Unlock the power of AI. Dominate the LinkedIn competition. Start your training today!

Product Recommendation

pipedrive™

THE BEST CRM FOR SALES

Pipedrive is the sales-focused CRM trusted by over 100,000 companies worldwide. Voted the easiest to use, it features seamless integrations, customizable pipelines, and powerful reporting to help you close more deals, faster. Stay organized and ahead with Pipedrive!

Get a 30-day free trial right here: (Offer subject to change)

Mailbox
POWER

Birthday
MEMBERSHIP

Make a Huge Impact With Those You Care About
By Sending Automatic Birthday Cards & Gifts.

Whether it be clients or loved ones, our easy-to-use system keeps track of all their birth dates, so you don't have to! When their special day is around the corner, we'll send out personalized cards or gifts that arrive just in time. Never miss a birthday again.

Easily Collect Addresses.
What if I don't have their address? No problem; your account includes an online address book with a unique link to you. Just share the link, and when your contact fills out the form, they'll be automatically added to your birthday campaign and you'll receive an SMS text notification.

Personalize Every Gift To Your Contacts Automatically.
No more handwriting cards one by one; using merge fields, our system will personalize each card & gift with your recipient's first name automatically. Now, you can make every one of your clients feel special without the hand cramps & paper cuts.

Send Custom Birthday Gifts With Any Budget.
Whether you want to send luxury gifts or send thoughtful cards on a budget, Mailbox Power has a vast selection of gifts that you can fully customize. You have full control of what you send, who you send it to, and how much you spend per gift.

It's your card.
We'll never put our brand on your cards. Each of your recipients will think you personally printed & mailed these cards yourself. You can add your own logo, photos, text, or create whatever design you desire. Each card is sent in a plain white premium envelope with a real stamp for authenticity!

Start Sending Today!

www.ingramcontent.com/pod-product-compliance
Lightning Source LLC
Chambersburg PA
CBHW031840200326
41597CB00012B/216